AF252091

Edited by Larry Richards
Introduction by Phyllis Lambert

Centre Canadien d'Architecture / Canadian Centre for Architecture

BUILDING AND GARDENS

Centre Canadien d'Architecture /
Canadian Centre for Architecture
Montréal, 1989

Distributed by The MIT Press
Cambridge, Massachusetts and London, England

© Centre Canadien d'Architecture /Canadian Centre for Architecture, Montréal, 1989

Library of Congress Cataloging-in-Publication data

Centre Canadien d'Architecture /Canadian Centre for Architecture
    building and gardens / edited by Larry Richards
    p.   cm
ISBN 0-920785-12-3. – ISBN 0-262-68058-0 (MIT Press)
1. Canadian Centre for Architecture. 2. Architecture, Modern – 20th century – Quebec (Province) – Montreal. 3. Montreal (Quebec) – Buildings, structures, etc. 4. Gardens – Quebec (Province) – Montreal.
I. Richards, Larry. II. Canadian Centre for Architecture
NA 2405.C2M664 1989   727′.7′09714281 – dc19   88-36968

Legal deposits: 2nd Quarter, 1989
Bibliothèque nationale du Québec
National Library of Canada

Issued also in French under the title *Centre Canadien d'Architecture / Canadian Centre for Architecture : Architecture et paysage*
(ISBN 0-920785-14-X)

This book, designed by Glenn Goluska, was typeset in Ehrhardt by The Coach House Press and printed and bound by Arthurs-Jones Lithographing Ltd. in Canada.

Copyright in works of art reproduced
Figs. 19, 20 © Gerrard and Mackars Landscape Architects; figs. 22, 28, 32, 34–37 © Melvin Charney; figs. 41, 50, 51, 52, pages 82–86 © Peter Rose Architect; page 81 © Peter Rose Architect and Melvin Charney.

Photograph credits
Front cover, pages 105-109, 116, Richard Pare; fig. 1, Jorgen Watz; figs. 8, 9, Geremy Butler; figs. 15, 38, 58, 67, 68, 69, pages 104, 110-115, 117, 118, Gabor Szilasi; pages 35, 54, Laura Volkerding; pages 36-39, 52, 53, David Miller; pages 40-51, Clara Gutsche; figs. 23, 56, Michel Boulet, CCA Photo Services; figs. 26, 33, Melvin Charney; fig. 30, Christopher Thacker; fig. 53 pages 70, 73, 75, 76, Alain Laforest, CCA Photo Services; figs. 40, 70, *La Presse*; fig. 54, 61-63, Richard Pare and Phyllis Lambert; fig. 65, Brian Merret; fig. 71, back cover, Geoffrey James. Copy photos by Michel Boulet and Alain Laforest, CCA Photo Services.

Contents

Preface

In 1986 the Canadian Centre for Architecture invited me to edit a book and curate an exhibition about its new building in Montréal. Honoured to be given the opportunity to collaborate with the many individuals who were passionately engaged in creating this new institution, I also knew that the overlapping work on the book and exhibition would be complex.

The site and building were in early stages of construction; final design detailing was still in progress. From the hundreds of incomplete and not yet physically connected parts, it would be necessary to imagine an integrated whole – to visualize the completed CCA building and gardens as they would appear in 1989. Accepting this unique position of being both a recorder of an existing history and participant in a story which was continuing to unfold, I began the dual process of studying the institution's past while experiencing the reality of the emerging architecture.

By winter 1987 I was immersed in the vast quantity of material documenting the planning, design, and construction of the CCA. Nearly a decade's worth of correspondence, proposals, reports, contracts, and visual material – most of it in the CCA archives and the office of the architect Peter Rose – had to be assimilated. I observed the new construction and the restoration of the Shaughnessy House. I studied the materials and finishes, the qualities of the spaces and changing light. I talked with a broad cross-section of those who were shaping the building and gardens: designers, consultants, supervisors, workers.

As a result of this immersion, institutional and architectural issues began to emerge, and the broad outlines of the book began to take shape. Authors were selected along with modes of expression appropriate to the recounting and making of the CCA story. As well, it became clear that it was essential to explore more general questions related to architecture and urban environments in the late twentieth century.

The research for and production of this book involved many dedicated individuals who maintained collective attention to the concept and the details. The Exhibitions and Publications department of the CCA was responsible for the book under the steady guidance of curator Eva Blau. Cynthia Ware, publications manager until October 1988, brought an additional intellectual dimension to the book. Esther Beaudry, who succeeded Cynthia Ware as publications manager, expertly coordinated the production of the French edition. Beaudry and I worked closely with project editor Francesca Worrall whose attention to detail was invaluable. Brooke Hodge, exhibitions coordinator, and Helen Malkin, curatorial assistant of Exhibitions and Publications, were involved in both the book and the accompanying exhibition from the start. They assumed key roles in the organization of the related projects. Ai Tsuzuki assisted with gathering research material; and Jocelyne Gervais and Marthe Vary did the very demanding word processing for the text. This core group ensured that the English and French versions of the book would be produced carefully and on time for the 1989 opening.

The writers and interview participants were enormously cooperative: my appreciation goes to Phyllis Lambert, John Harris, Chantal Pontbriand, George Baird, Peter Rose, and Melvin Charney for their thoughtful contributions. Alan Stewart and Brian Young researched the early history of the site. Robert Lemire of the CCA Archives developed the site chronology, for which cartographer Daniel Thibault executed the maps. Helen Malkin compiled the final section of information on the building and gardens. Special thanks must go to the copy editors: Monick Élie for the French edition and Stephanie Jones for the English edition; to the translators, Robert Paquin, Catherine Roberge, and Micheline Sainte-Marie; and to Alberto Perez-Gomez who

reviewed the manuscript as external reader. I also thank Glenn Goluska who designed the book with particular care, generating an elegant statement of his own.

Many people were involved in producing and selecting photographs for the book. David Harris, assistant curator of photographs, was always helpful; his finely tuned visual sense was important to the selection process. Members of the CCA Photo Services, Alain Laforest and Michel Boulet, assisted by Yves Eigenmann, devoted many hours to photographing the building during construction phases; they assisted me in seeing beyond the surface. Richard Pare, consultant to the photographs collection, contributed exquisite photographs as did the guest photographers whose work was commissioned by the CCA: Clara Gutsche, Geoffrey James, David Miller, Gabor Szilasi, and Laura Volkerding.

The accompanying exhibition, "Centre Canadien d'Architecture / Canadian Centre for Architecture: Building and Gardens," includes a video by the Montreal film makers, ZONE PRODUCTIONS. The video concept matured during 1987–88 through an extensive study of how to capture the space and time of the CCA in moving images. This activity paralleled work on the book and generated new insights which influenced my experience of the building and the direction of the book.

Throughout, I talked with and learned from Peter Rose, architect of the CCA. Our intensive discussions about the conceptual basis of the design, about materiality and tectonics, and about Montreal were integral to the book's development. I appreciate the assistance I received from Peter Rose's associates who were intimately involved in the design and realization of the building: Nicholas Garrison, Erik Marosi, and Bill Steinberg. Rose's office was responsible for the portfolio of ink-line drawings of the site and building – precise work executed by Gregory Henriquez in conjunction with Jill Alexander, David Kepron, and Marie-Paule Macdonald.

All of this collaborative activity by a large group of people was enthusiastically driven by Phyllis Lambert, director of the CCA. She communicated to me a grand, consistent vision of a dynamic whole wherein a building, its gardens and the books, drawings, and photographs it contains "talk to" and mirror one another. The essays and illustrations in this book combine to reveal her understanding of the potential of a museum of architecture as a statement: about the nature of the works it collects and exhibits; about its role in the life of a culture or a city; about architecture itself.

Now that the building and gardens are nearly complete, memories of the complicated process leading to the realization of this distinctive new place in Montréal begin to fade. I trust that this book will preserve some of the essential traces of creative thought and action which culminated in the Canadian Centre for Architecture.

The University of Waterloo generously granted a sabbatical for 1988 which enabled my work as editor and curator at the CCA. Finally, I thank my friends in Toronto and Waterloo who supported me throughout this most rewarding project.

LARRY RICHARDS
January 1989

Note to the reader: In 1988 Boulevard Dorchester was renamed Boulevard René-Lévesque. In certain instances the name Boulevard Dorchester is retained to maintain historical accuracy.

Introduction

The Centre Canadien d'Architecture / Canadian Centre for Architecture was founded in 1979 as an independent study centre and museum to further the understanding of architecture and to help establish architecture as a public concern, both for those with little or no knowledge of the building arts, and for those who are most instrumental in shaping knowledge through research. Within this general goal the CCA was formed to further scholarship, to encourage informed participation in decisions about the future of cities and their buildings; and to foster interchange among architects, historians, preservationists, and the general public.

The CCA's research and public programmes are based on its collections of drawings, prints, books, photographs, and architectural archives. The library includes, at this writing, 120,000 volumes on the history, theory, and practice of architecture, world wide; and on related subjects such as landscape architecture, building technology, and urban planning. Its holdings range from fifteenth-century imprints to the present.

The prints and drawings holdings of some 20,000 works encompass the same scope and include projects built and theoretical, generated by practice, study, travel, and competition. They represent work not only by architects but also by artists who influenced architectural thinking, visionaries, interior designers, engineers, sculptor architects, and designers for the stage.

The CCA archives, predominantly North American in emphasis, now number more than a quarter of a million items representing the work and working tools of individual architects and firms: drawings, specifications, models, travel sketches, account books, and entire libraries. The CCA archives hold such records of architects and planners who worked across Canada in the first half of the twentieth century, as well as contemporary architects who have worked internationally.

The photographs collection, which comprises approximately 40,000 historical images, is in the size and quality of its holdings, one of the major collections of photographs anywhere, and its focus on the subject of architecture is unique. The collection provides a comprehensive history of the medium as related to architecture, from the announcement of the invention of photography in 1839 to the present. It represents both well-known photographers and anonymous recorders of architectural subjects. In addition to collecting, the photographs department also commissions projects.

Since its founding the CCA has worked to develop modes of access to its collections, creating an integrated database that will make it possible, using a single access point based in the CCA library, to search across all types of material in the collections – books and periodicals, prints and drawings, photographs, archives – singly, in combination, or collectively. This access is extended beyond the CCA through participation in international information networks, including the Research Library Information Network, and the Foundation for Documents of Architecture, which seeks to provide access to architectural records world wide by promoting the development of databases and networks, and scholarly standards for automated cataloguing.

Exhibitions prepared by the CCA in its first five years include *Photography and Architecture: 1839–1939*, drawn from the CCA's photographs collections, which travelled to museums in Europe and North America in 1982–84; and *Les villas de Pline et les éléments classiques dans l'architecture à Montréal*, at the Musée des beaux-arts in Montréal (1983), based on an exhibition which originated at the Institut Français d'Architecture in Paris. The CCA's publications include *Photography and Architecture: 1839–1939*, by Richard Pare, published in connection with the exhibition; *Planned Assaults* (1987), by Lars Lerup; *Ernest Isbell Barott, Architect* (1985), by Susan Wagg; a series of pamphlet guides to the architecture of Montréal; and guides to collections in the CCA archives.

These are accomplishments of the relatively sheltered years of planning and development. Now, with its opening, the CCA becomes an active study centre and museum serving a contemporary public. The locus of this new life is the building, whose design and realization have been integral to the CCA's formation as an institution. Thus it seems particularly appropriate to inaugurate the CCA as an architectural museum and study centre with an exhibition and publication about the building that houses it. (A parallel exhibition and publication, *Architecture and Its Image*, focuses on the CCA collections.)

The publication *Centre Canadien d'Architecture / Canadian Centre for Architecture: Building and Gardens* accompanies the exhibition of the same name, curated by Larry Richards. The book presents the CCA building and gardens in written contributions, photographs, and drawings. Each contributor articulates, either as a protagonist or a critic, the ideas which generated the design of the building and landscape.

The essays and the interview that make up the central chapters present the viewpoints of the principals: Peter Rose, the architect; Melvin Charney, the garden architect; and myself, the client and consulting architect. These three chapters address the major aspects of design, but each is necesarily incomplete: as is true of the building and gardens which are their subject, layers of ideas criss-cross each other to build the greater whole. The introductory and concluding essays are contextual and critical. An essay by John Harris, on the origins of architectural museums, opens the volume. The urban history of the quartier that includes the CCA, prepared by Robert Lemire and presented in a series of maps and images, ends it. Larry Richards's discussion of the building provides both a critique and an overview.

Photographs of construction and restoration (black and white) by Clara Gutsche, David Miller, and Laura Volkerding, and of the almost completed building (colour) by Richard Pare and Gabor Szilasi bracket the central section of the book. The photographs, made with large-format cameras in available light, were commissioned by the CCA as part of a visual and written archive documenting all aspects of the building – from the initial design concept through the successive phases of restoration and construction. The photographs are formal "portraits"; they are concerned with light, space, and architectonics. As David Harris, assistant curator of photographs has written, the black-and-white photographs show "the accidental and poignant beauty of the temporarily deserted buildings, with materials and tools set aside, and work stilled." Together with the colour photographs, they build from part to whole. The images of Pare and Szilasi seek to represent a balance between the conceptual and physical nature of architecture.

Larry Richards ends his analysis of the building with a vision of the collections, protected in their basement rooms: "Resting on their vanilla-coloured steel shelves, quietly and peacefully hidden from the expressway traffic speeding through tunnels only a few metres beyond their securing walls, one imagines the treasures to be telling stories. And I imagine that these stories are about a new future outside the walls – a place of restored architectural consciousness and community." "The point of the CCA," says Peter Rose in explaining certain aspects of the building's design, "is to get you to go back out with your newfound knowledge and look at the city." This relationship between "inside" and "outside," between the museum and the built world, underlies the concept – institutional and architectural – of the CCA. Thus, as this book attempts to outline, the CCA building seeks to be a place of discourse, a literate architecture that is part of the contradictions and realities of the city and of history.

PHYLLIS LAMBERT
Montréal, August 1988.

Storehouses of Knowledge:
The Origins of the Contemporary
Architectural Museum

JOHN HARRIS

The history of architectural museums is a contemporary subject.[1] At the International Conference of Architectural Museums, held in Helsinki in 1979, there was lively debate as to which was the first such museum. (The A.V. Chusev Museum in Moscow, founded in 1934, claimed some priority.) One left the conference with an ambiguous view of what constitutes an architectural museum. Not the least cause of the ambiguity was the diverse character of the institutions that could claim membership in this new union. Represented in the International Confederation of Architectural Museums (ICAM) today are libraries (Avery Architectural Library, Columbia University, New York), academies (Royal Danish Academy of Fine Arts, Copenhagen), technical universities (the Architektursammlung, Munich), professional architectural institutions (Royal Institute of British Architects, London), schools of architecture (Architectural Association, London), and so-called architectural museums (Swedish Museum of Architecture, Stockholm). Indeed, when ICAM was founded after the Helsinki conference, the word *confederation* replaced *union* to reflect the variety of the member institutions.

If the Centre Canadien d'Architecture / Canadian Centre for Architecture is to be seen in context, it is first necessary to identify the typical components of some modern architectural museums. Those in Helsinki, Stockholm, and Wroclaw may be used as prototypes. The Museum of Finnish Architecture was founded in 1949, the Swedish Museum of Architecture in 1962, and the Museum of Architecture in Wroclaw in 1965. Each occupies an historic building that has been adapted to house a collection of architectural drawings by the nation's architects, a library, a lecture room, an exhibition gallery, and a photographic archive. The collections may include photographs, models, architectural fragments or casts, artifacts such as furniture, and drawing instruments.

Other such institutions are not called architectural museums, but their components are the same. Examples include the Burnham Library of Architecture of the Art Institute of Chicago, founded in 1912 as a result of Daniel Burnham's bequest and merged in the 1960s with the Art Institute's Ryerson Library; the Royal Institute of British Architects (RIBA), especially the Drawings Collection established in Portman Square in 1970; the collection of the University of Warsaw; and that of the Royal Danish Academy of Fine Arts, where a drawings collection and library serve a teaching establishment (fig. 1).

These institutions have been enriched over the years by the gifts of architects who wished to preserve all or part of their own collections. Daniel Burnham is a good example. As he was trained in the Beaux-Arts tradition, he collected exemplars by other architects or mentors, and these passed with his own drawings and library to the library named after him. Burnham (and hence the library) had material of predominantly eighteenth- and nineteenth-century origins. The collections of the University of Warsaw, the Royal Danish Academy, and the RIBA also include pre-twentieth-century material and so have a more international or historical flavour than do the more recently founded institutions in Helsinki and Stockholm, where modern and national collections have been formed. (It ought to be said that architectural collections of early formation are also to be found in traditional museums such as the Victoria and Albert Museum in London, the Musée des arts décoratifs in Paris, the Uffizi in Florence, and, not least, the Cooper-Hewitt Museum, the Smithsonian Institution's National Museum of Design in New York.[2] Most of these institutions are not, strictly speaking, architectural museums; their architectural collections are part of a complex whole. Nevertheless, they have large holdings and, particularly in the case of the Cooper-Hewitt, active architectural exhibition programmes.)

fig. 1   Study room in Royal Danish Academy of Fine Arts, Copenhagen. Photograph: Jorgen Watz, 1987. Academy of Fine Arts Library, Copenhagen.

Some modern architectural museums have domestic origins. The Llubljana Museum is, in fact, the house and office of Josef Plecnik (who died in 1957); it contains his own architectural drawings, his library, the drawing office and studio, some models, pictures, and photographs, and various art works or artifacts. Llubljana is essentially a microcosm of the public architectural museums of Helsinki, Stockholm, and Wroclaw. In the future, Llubljana will expand and become a proper state architectural museum; however, its origins will still be in the house and office of Plecnik, just as the origins of the Burnham Library can be traced back to the office of Burnham and Root in the Rookery Building, and beyond that to a studio in Burnham's house. Components of these two institutions vary, but essentially they are extensions of the architectural office that occupied part of the architect's dwelling, to which has been grafted an exhibition gallery and a lecture room. This can be described as the domestic prototype for the architectural museum.

Both Burnham and Plecnik surrounded themselves with tools of reference. The modern architectural museum is a tool of reference on a large scale. Therefore it is inviting to review the history of architectural tools of reference.

Every architect needs to collect tools of reference, even if only a sketchbook or a few humble printed pattern books. Sketchbooks have served this purpose; early examples include that of Villard de Honnecourt in which he recorded details seen in his travels. Early sixteenth-century architects compiled what can be described as portable museums of architectural elements and details, particularly of the classical orders. These were important tools because there was then no encyclopedic collection, or printed museum as such, apart from A. Lafreri's *Speculum Romanae Magnificentiae*, a miscellaneous collection of engraved views and details of ancient Rome. A famous early eighteenth-century example is Bernard de Montfaucon's *L'Antiquité expliquée*, published in five volumes in 1719 and five in 1724. In scope, Montfaucon's work was preceded by Pirro Ligorio's illustrated anthology of antiquity, which had grown to forty volumes by 1553, but which was never published. Ligorio was exceptional; the norm was the individual sketchbook, such as *Il Taccuino Senese* of Giuliano da Sangallo the elder (ca. 1488–1513); the Bernardo della Volpaia Codex Coner (ca. 1495–1510); or the sketchbook of Villard de Honnecourt, mentioned above. Cassiano dal Pozzo's vast collection of draw-

ings, completed between 1620 and 1650, was later called a "paper museum" or Museum Chartaceum.[3] Thus did the modern architectural museum evolve from the paper museum of three centuries ago. It is from these beginnings that the encyclopedic museological collection of post-revolutionary France emerged.

A less portable method of architectural reference was found in the walls of gardens and courtyards used as a vehicle for the display of fragments and ornamental sculpture; for example, the Palazzi Farnese and the Mattei in Rome. Principally, these were aesthetic evocations. The fragments were not organized or catalogued, and we do not know if renaissance architects saw these ambiences as repositories of knowledge. Many were purely decorative or were means of conserving antique fragments, pieces of sarcophagi and cornices excavated from a site as a result of new building. Nevertheless, it is important that they were displayed, and some architects may have seen them as storehouses of knowledge. In the later eighteenth century these ambiences were probably endowed with more historical significance than they had been originally.

We do not know how renaissance architects physically arranged their offices or studios. The evidence has not survived, but we may suppose that Serlio, Palladio, or Le Vau occupied rooms not so different from Sir William Chambers's 1760s office in Berners Street, London. At the end of his garden was a collection of rooms housing his drawing office, where his assistants and apprentices worked; his library; and his portfolios or cupboards of architectural designs, and a variety of architectural paraphernalia. Absent from Chambers's studio was a collection of designs by other architects acquired for historical or stylistic reasons.

Before the consolidation of the Beaux-Arts training tradition, architects kept their own designs and may have acquired a few by other architects, especially by the architects who had trained them – as Serlio acquired the designs of his master, Peruzzi; Scamozzi those of Palladio; or John Webb those of Inigo Jones.[4] The first evidence we have of an architect acquiring architectural designs by another architect as a trophy or an act of homage is Inigo Jones's 1614 purchase, from Scamozzi, or Palladio's family, of Palladio's designs for public and private buildings.[5]

An architect's collection of drawings, comprising his own designs plus miscellaneous others, is very different from an architectural drawings collection that has been assembled with a plan in mind. This distinction is important because architectural drawings have begun to feature prominently in the composition of the modern architectural museum. From the early eighteenth century the container, the building, was often still domestic in type and scale, but in a few pioneering cases the collection was organized as it might be in a modern drawings cabinet.

The idea of a paper museum of architectural designs became a reality around 1700, with two remarkable pairs of father-and-son architect / collectors: in Stockholm, Nicodemus Tessin the elder (1615–81) and younger (1654–1728), and in London, William (1650–1719) and John (1677–1726) Talman. The Tessins' substantial collection of mainly French architectural, decorative, ornamental, and garden designs is housed today in the Nationalmuseum, Stockholm.[6] It was amassed by the Tessins, both of whom consecutively held the post of superintendent of Swedish Royal Building. Tessin the younger was succeeded by Carl Harleman from 1728 and Carl Johan Cronstedt from 1753, both of whom added to the initial Tessin collection, which even then included over two hundred designs for Versailles alone. Nevertheless, there is no information on how the Tessins kept their drawings, or if they were separate from those for the Swedish Royal Works. What is relevant is that the Tessins collected French exemplars to aid their own design work, and in this they were acting little differently from Beaux-Arts architects like Destailleur or Burnham.[7]

The Talman collection is quite another matter, for not only was it then the largest known gathering of books, prints, and drawings of architecture (it contained many old master drawings as well), but it seems to have been assembled with the idea of a museum in mind. By 1700 William Talman had acquired the Palladio corpus, to which had been added most of the designs by Inigo Jones and John Webb. (The whole is now known as the Burlington-Devonshire Collection of the Royal Institute of British Architects.) John Talman, William's son, was intent upon commissioning Italian artists to record altar-pieces, decoration, and church plate and vestments; to all these were added sculptures, paintings, objects of art, and some architectural fragments. In

William's day, all was kept in London, but after his death in 1719, John removed the collection to his home in the country. Interestingly, John attempted to classify his drawings with a system of code numbers and symbols, proof of museological intent, and about 1710 he made several designs for a country house in which to display the collection (fig. 2).[8]

The idea of a Talman museum might have been the father's, for it is significant that soon after William's death, John sold what became the Burlington-Devonshire Collection to Richard Boyle, third Earl of Burlington. He sold the Jones-Webb drawings in 1720 and those by Palladio in 1721.

Lord Burlington, soon to distinguish himself as the "architect earl" and the most professional of all amateur architects, was the first architect who, by search and purchase, formed a collection of architectural designs of international (although predominantly Italian) origin. His collection was not only a tool of reference for his own use; it was also used by his assistants, was most likely available to the more senior members of the Office of Works, and was seen as part of a programme he initiated to educate taste and spread the gospel of neo-Palladianism. This was backed up by his publication and promotion of at least four neo-Palladian books. Burlington was also commissioning or acquiring measured drawings, a tradition that goes back to the time of Giuliano da Sangallo the elder, who is known to have commissioned drawings of existing buildings. As early as 1719, Burlington had already been reported as planning to employ architects to measure buildings in the Veneto, a precursor, even if abortive, of Antonio Visentini's huge programme of producing sets of measured drawings of Palladian buildings.

Burlington used the Bagnio or Casina in the gardens of Chiswick House as a drawing office, outside the door of which appropriately stood the statues of Palladio and Jones. After the new villa was built in 1726, his books and drawings were kept in the library on the main floor, but it is unclear if his office was in the villa or in Burlington House in London. Two "chests of drawers" are mentioned in the library, but it is improbable that these were the sort of plan chest that we find in Sir John Soane's Museum.[9]

There were other repositories before and after 1700 in which a mass of architectural drawings might have composed a paper

fig. 2 Section of John Talman's proposed library showing book presses, ca. 1710. By courtesy of the Board of Trustees of the Victoria and Albert Museum.

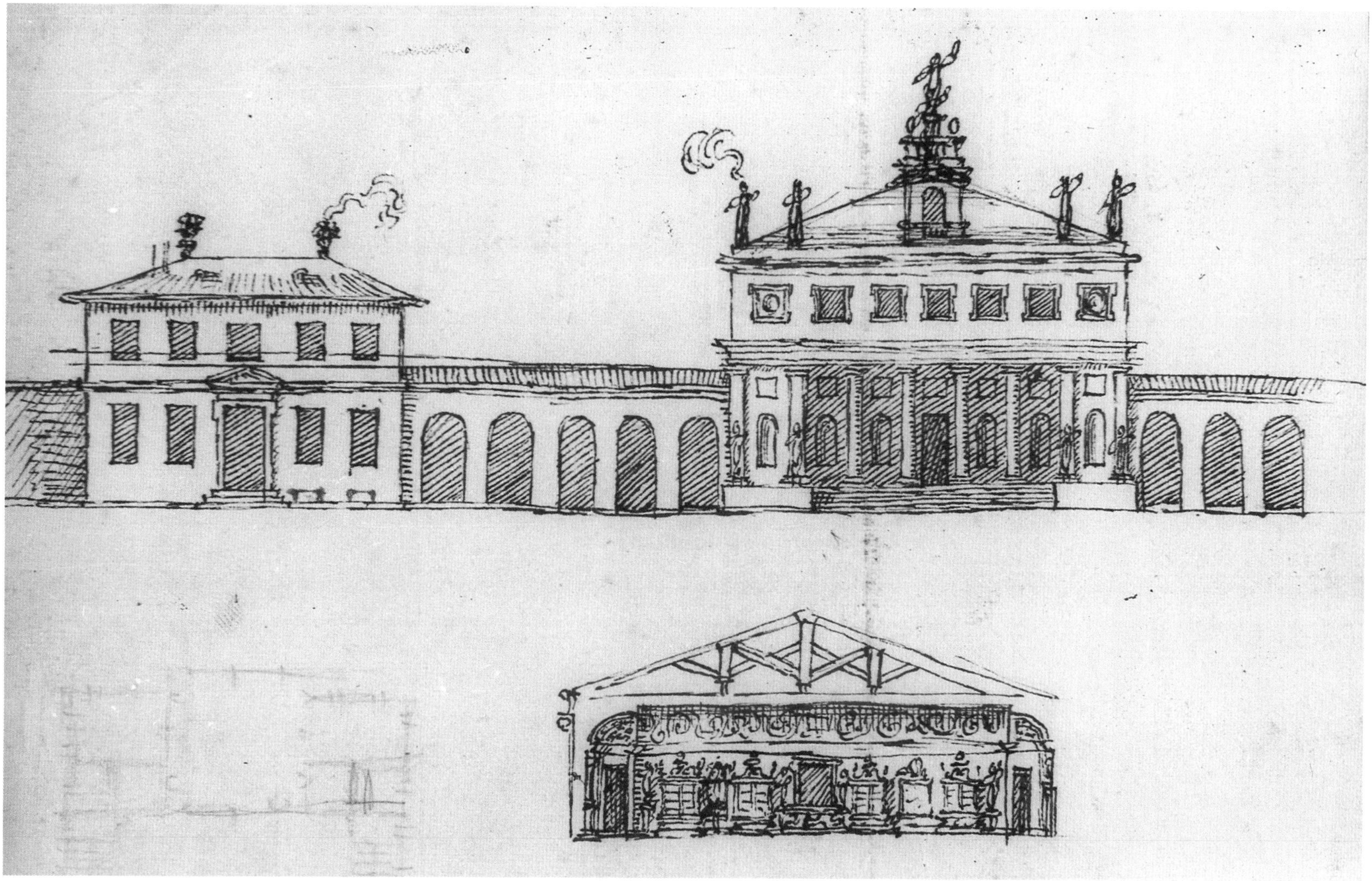

fig. 3 Interior perspective design for a paper repository, probably for the Office of Works. Engraving attributed to Nicholas Hawksmoor, 1715. Department of Prints, The Metropolitan Museum of Art, Harris Brisbane Dick Fund, 1926 (26.85 p. 234 vo).

fig. 4 John Talman's design for a paper repository for the government papers of the Exchequer, today the Public Record Office. Reproduced from Thomas Maddox, *Antiquus Dialogus*, 1711. By permission of the British Library.

museum, albeit an embryonic one. In France, a large accumulation of drawings belonged to the Bâtiments du Roi, housed in the Louvre;[10] and in England there was the Office of Works, in old Whitehall Palace. In 1716, the Office Room in Whitehall was rebuilt or refashioned internally by Nicholas Hawksmoor to include "Conveniencys for the Clerks and Officekeeper, together with Closetts, Presses &c for repositing the Books, Drawings & Designs belonging to the several Palaces."[11] Divided between the Metropolitan Museum of Art and Sir John Soane's Museum are two designs that could be Hawksmoor's own for one of these rooms (fig. 3).[12] The shelves of what at first appears to be a library are in fact of some depth in order to take rolls of drawings, as in the design John Talman made before 1711 for a room for storing the papers of the Exchequer, then London's equivalent to Paris's Archives nationales (fig. 4).[13]

As was also true of academies of art, a building designed specifically as a repository for architectural documents, or indeed for architectural activity, was not considered necessary.[14] The Royal Academy in Somerset House, London (1776), presented an opportunity to design rooms for specific purposes; yet even when the fabric was new, the rooms were not purpose-built for their functions. Somerset House, Chambers's masterpiece, was a unique achievement, as indeed was the idea of uniting various public offices under a common roof, yet the rooms used for the Life Class, the Antique School, the Painting School, the Library, or the Architecture Room all might just as well have been bedrooms or saloons as far as the shape or decoration was suited to their purposes. Only the Great Exhibition Room was specifically designed for the public display of paintings and drawings, and this specificity was unusual, although not unique, in 1776.[15]

On the whole, it was the same for the storage of drawings in university collections, for although methods of book storage had developed over the centuries, drawings in university and college collections (and likewise cathedral collections) were generally kept haphazardly in libraries, as is well demonstrated by the history of architectural drawings in Oxbridge collections. The best that could be expected was to be found in the library of St. John's College, Oxford, where seventeenth-century muniment cupboards provided a long drawer at the bottom for maps of estates and presumably architectural designs.[16]

Despite the fact that historians have studied the development of hierarchical planning in royal palaces and the greater houses – what the French appropriately call *distribution* – no comparable attention has been focused on the planning of museums and academies in the eighteenth century. Although the Museum Fredericianum at Kassel (1769) has been considered one of the first (if not the first) purpose-built museums, it is often forgotten that designs for a British Museum were being prepared in 1754. These designs by Cornelius Johnson and John Vardy, might, however, have served as easily for a royal palace. The same is true of a museum design by J.P. Gisors that won first prize in the 1779 Grand Prix competition, for E.-C. Boullée's megalomaniacally scaled museum proposed in 1783, and for many later designs.[17]

The history of the planning and furnishing of academies is a fruitful field of research that might throw light on the practical training of the architect as well as on the history of the architectural museum. At the Royal Academy of Arts in London, the annual exhibition of members' work included a section on architecture, at first mixed with the other art exhibits, but later, in the 1790s, displayed in a special Architecture Room. For the most part paper designs were displayed, and many who visited these shows must have ruminated on the problem of displaying architecture, of bringing inside some idea of what is an outside subject.[18]

Events in the late 1700s led to the development in Paris of new approaches to the use of architectural models for pedagogical exhibition.[19] One stimulus was renewed attention to the ancient world. Throughout the second half of the eighteenth century, architects studied ancient monuments by measuring them and confirming or disputing earlier authorities such as Palladio or Antoine Desgodets. This activity led to the making of casts of parts of famous buildings and of architectural models. This was the first step toward the creation of a museum of architecture.

Some of the earliest models are carved in cork by Augusto Rosa (1738–84), whose Temple of Neptune in the École des Beaux-Arts is dated 1777. There was also Giovanni Altieri, whose Temple of Vesta at Tivoli in Sir John Soane's Museum is also dated 1777. By about 1800 the making of cork models was principally in the hands of Antonio Chichi (1743–1816), who had also started his workshop in the 1770s.[20]

Concurrent with this activity was the production of plaster of Paris models, by 1800 mostly by J.P. Fouquet, whose "modèles d'architecture pour l'instruction des élèves" of the École Royale Polytechnique and the École des Ponts-et-Chaussées frequently appear in accounts (such as in 1816). Fouquet is important in this context because he had made many of the models in the Cassas Gallery.[21]

This model-making cannot be discussed without reference to the making of casts of capitals and fragments of ancient buildings. In 1790 Guillaume Couture went to Italy to cast capitals and ornaments to aid craftsmen in Paris, and in 1786 the Comte de Choiseul-Gouffier was supervising casts made in Greece. Léon Dufourny in Sicily was assembling a collection of casts, cork models, and fragments. These pioneers knew each other, and in their minds later, if not then, was the problem of presenting architecture, of translating the paper museum into a three-dimensional one.

Couture, Choiseul-Gouffier, and Dufourny were all perfectly aware that Alexandre Lenoir was bringing together, in the Louvre's depot in the old convent of the Petits-Augustins in the rue des Petits-Augustins, architectural fragments and larger elements of Gothic architecture. It was really a museum of sculpture: Lenoir called it the musée des Monuments français. The twelve editions of the catalogue that appeared between 1793 and 1816 demonstrate that it was the first museum of architecture, if by museum is meant an arrangement of bits and pieces set about in a period ambience. Lenoir's museum was the ultimate extension of the fragments on the wall of renaissance courtyards, although his fragments were medieval rather than classical. In Lenoir's mind was the problem of how architecture should serve the public, in the way that the new musée du Louvre was presenting painting, sculpture, and objects of art. It is difficult today to reconstruct this type of ambience, but its flavour can best be experienced by a visit to the musée des Monuments français – now in the palais de Chaillot, but originally assembled by Viollet-le-Duc in 1879, or

fig. 5 The Cassas Gallery in the rue de Seine, Paris. Engraving: Bonvalet, drawing: Bance, 1806. Département des estampes, Bibliothèque Nationale, Paris (AA3 Bonvalet).

to such surviving collections of casts as in the cast courts of the Victoria and Albert Museum.

Couture, Choiseul-Gouffier, Dufourny, Lenoir – to these must be added the name of Louis-François Cassas, whose large collection of models and measured drawings of world architecture was exhibited publicly from 1806 in adapted accommodations, but with a purpose-designed *galerie des chefs d'oeuvres de l'architecture des différents peuples* (fig. 5). The Cassas gallery was something of a catalyst. An official commission was set up by A.T.L. Vaudoyer and J.N.L. Durand in 1808 to which Dufourny reported, proposing that the casts and models compose a *musée complet d'architecture*, the first recorded use of the term *museum of architecture*. J.G. Legrand's *Essai sur l'histoire générale de l'architecture* (1799) had already proposed a department of architecture for the Louvre in which architecture, painting, and sculpture would be integrated. This developed into the Legrand-Molinos scheme to make casts and fragments into an encyclopedic panorama of architecture, in which the idea of chronology and development of style was paramount. What Legrand and Jacques Molinos had accumulated was exhibited in an adapted house, 6, rue Saint-Florentin, and soon abandoned.

At this point, Sir John Soane enters the story. In the Legrand catalogue of 1806 in Soane's library, he marked in pencil Legrand's suggestion that models are the only way to exhibit architecture.[22] His drawing of 25 June 1808 for the remodelling of the Dome

fig. 6 Plan and partial section of Soane's lower office at 12 Lincoln's Inn Fields, showing proposed fitments and furniture, 1792. By courtesy of the Trustees of Sir John Soane's Museum, London.

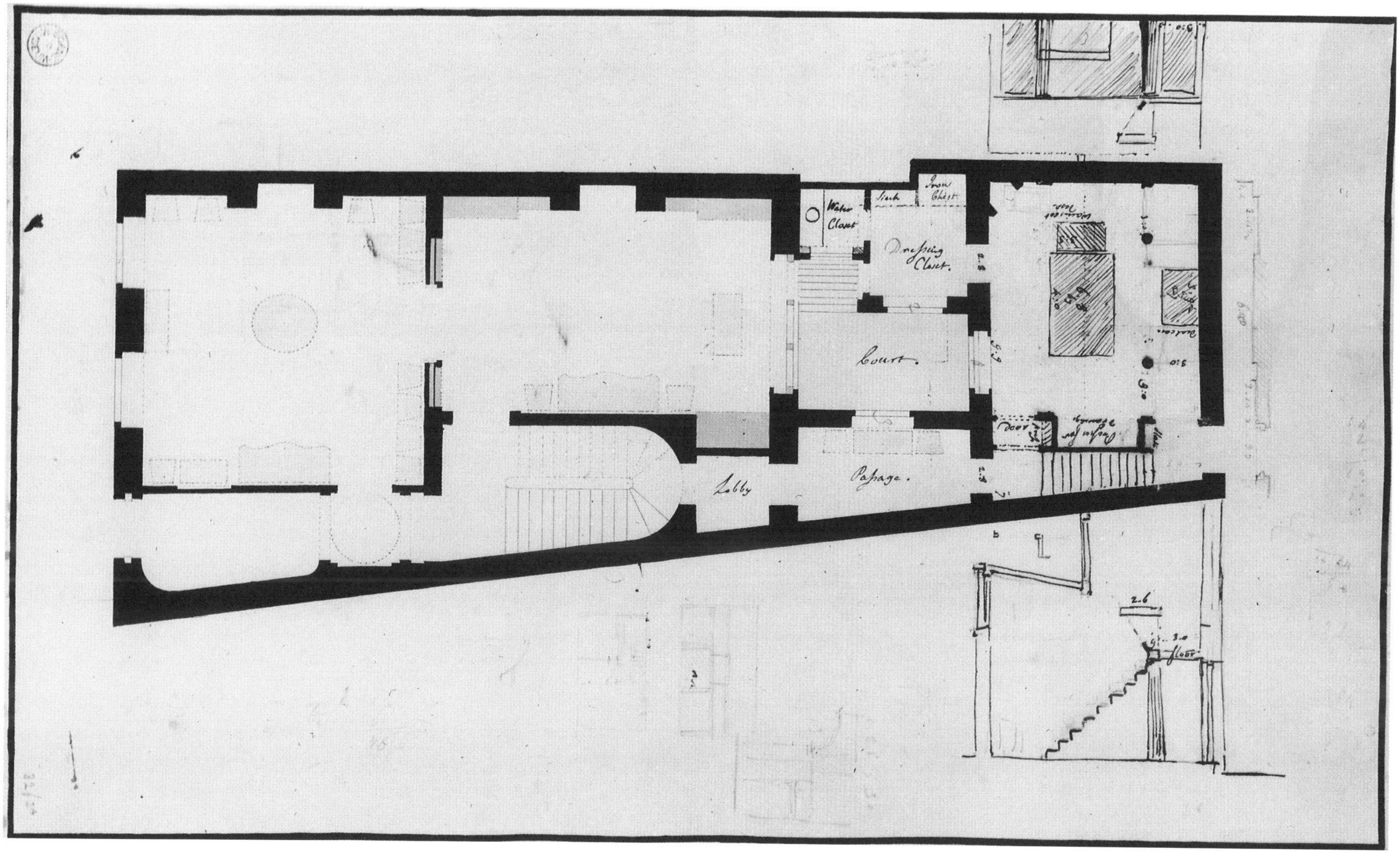

fig. 7 Soane's lower office. Drawing: James Adams, 1808. By courtesy of the Trustees of Sir John Soane's Museum.

Area in his house at numbers 12 and 13 Lincoln's Inn Fields – where he was to display, through two open floors, all his architectural fragments – is inscribed Design for the Museum (fig. 6).[23] There can be little doubt that from 1808, if not earlier, Soane arranged his collection with an eye to public display (fig. 7). Although house and office were combined in his two buildings, they were seen as one – a "union of architecture, sculpture and painting," to use the title of John Britton's book on the museum (1827). In Soane's museum are paintings, drawings, engravings, books, bronzes, terracottas, ancient and modern sculpture, architectural fragments, casts, models, large drawings of architecture,

fig. 8 Soane's upper office. Photograph: Geremy Butler, 1987. By courtesy of the Trustees of Sir John Soane's Museum.

fig. 9 Plan chest of ca. 1808, similar to those seen in early views of Soane's rooms, shown next to a modern plan chest for comparison. Photograph: Geremy Butler, 1987. By courtesy of the Trustees of Sir John Soane's Museum.

fig. 10 Soane's model room as installed by ca. 1825. Reproduced from John Britton, *Illustrations of the Public Buildings of London,* 1825–27. By courtesy of the Trustees of Sir John Soane's Museum.

and various objets d'art. By "union" was meant an homogenous and aesthetic arrangement of effects and collections within a specially designed container. Although the museum was planned on a small scale, and was a private initiative, Legrand would have acknowledged a fellow traveller on the same road to the architectural museum.[24]

The complexity and idiosyncrasies of Soane's renovations are not central to this discussion. What matters is that he was trying to assemble in his house all the elements of the architectural museum. His office contains, as far as we know, the earliest surviving plan chest of what is still the standard type (figs. 8, 9).

Soane's model stand in the Model Room, set up in 1828, provides storage in its lower part where half a dozen open flat drawers on runners can house very large drawings (fig. 10). The Dance Cabinet, containing drawings by George Dance acquired by Soane after Dance's death in 1825, is a standard plan chest set up on a stand designed by Soane as a sort of icon of veneration, but it is of uncertain date, and may postdate Soane's 1808 chests.

In arranging the various objects in his house, Soane was faced with the problem of having inadequate space. This may have led him to invent open-hanging wall storage in the picture cabinet. The idea of an encyclopedic display must also have been uppermost in his mind, and he may have seen his house as a storehouse of architectural knowledge. This knowledge was enshrined not only in his library, but in the architectural drawings collection that he formed. Like Burlington before him, he acquired large groups of drawings by those architects whom he either saw as his masters or his mentors, such as Chambers, Dance the younger, and Robert Adam. To these he added many more by a variety of architects: Kent's designs for the Houses of Parliament, Italian renaissance treatises, all sorts of sketchbooks, in infinite variety.

As far as we know, the only architect between Soane and Burlington who collected in this way was Robert Adam, who was concerned to record and collect evidence of ancient and modern architecture to facilitate his practice – and who was probably the first architect to organize an office in a modern way.[25] When Soane bought Robert Adam's drawings in 1833, these, together with the thousands of other drawings, the library, the model room, and the pictorial displays, made his museum a powerful tool of reference. It is often forgotten that Soane's is the only architectural library to have survived in situ since the renaissance.

In Soane's museum, the modern architectural museum has nearly been anticipated. It lacks only two features: a room devoted to the temporary or public display of pictures or drawings (an exhibition gallery), and a lecture room. As far as the gallery is concerned, Soane saw no need for one – for him the Royal Academy of Art was the proper venue for architects and students to annually display their designs.

Sir John Soane's Museum acquired public status on 20 April 1833, when an act of Parliament was passed "for settling and preserving" the museum. This act required appointed trustees to give free access to the museum on "at least two days every week throughout the months of April, May and June, and at such other times as the said trustees shall direct, to Amateurs and Students in Painting, Sculpture and Architecture … for consulting and benefitting by the said Collection."[26] Legally, the house was now open to the public and was a museum proper. After Soane's death in 1837, the visitors averaged as many as seventy a day.

The Royal Institute of British Architects, founded a few years before Soane died, steadily acquired the components of the modern architectural museum. Beginning in the early 1790s, architects met to consider the formation of an institute in London to represent the profession.[27] The Architects' Club came first; then in 1831 an Architectural Society was founded "to form a British School of Architecture, with the advantage of a Library, Museum, Professorships, and periodical exhibitions." It met in adapted accommodations in Exeter Hall off the Strand. George Moore's evocative "View of a Room … arranged at a *conversazione*" pro-

fig.11 *"View of a Room … arranged at a conversazione"* of the "museum" of the Architectural Society. George Moore, ca.1830. The British Architectural Library, RIBA.

vides a rare glimpse of this proto-museum (fig. 11).[28] Finally, in 1834, the Institute of British Architects (later the Royal Institute of British Architects) was founded. Thus, in England, unlike in France where state patronage continued to prevail, a professional body politic was being established to represent the architect in private practice.

The RIBA began to acquire the components of a museum, and from the beginning it was intent to build up not only a library, but also a collection of architectural drawings, acquiring as early as 1838 the famous Drummond-Stewart Collection of scenographic designs. Initially the RIBA was open only to members; it opened to the public on a limited basis after 1858. Not until 1934 did it occupy purpose-built accommodations – the first purpose-built repository and meeting place for a professional architectural institute in the world – with a modern library, an auditorium, exhibition halls, a restaurant, and supporting services (see fig. 12). However, no designed display space was provided for drawings, and drawings were not featured within the containership of the library as a subject for special treatment. With a little more luck and foresight, the RIBA might have had become the first proper architectural museum, had it not been a private members' institution. The character of its old quarters in what had been James

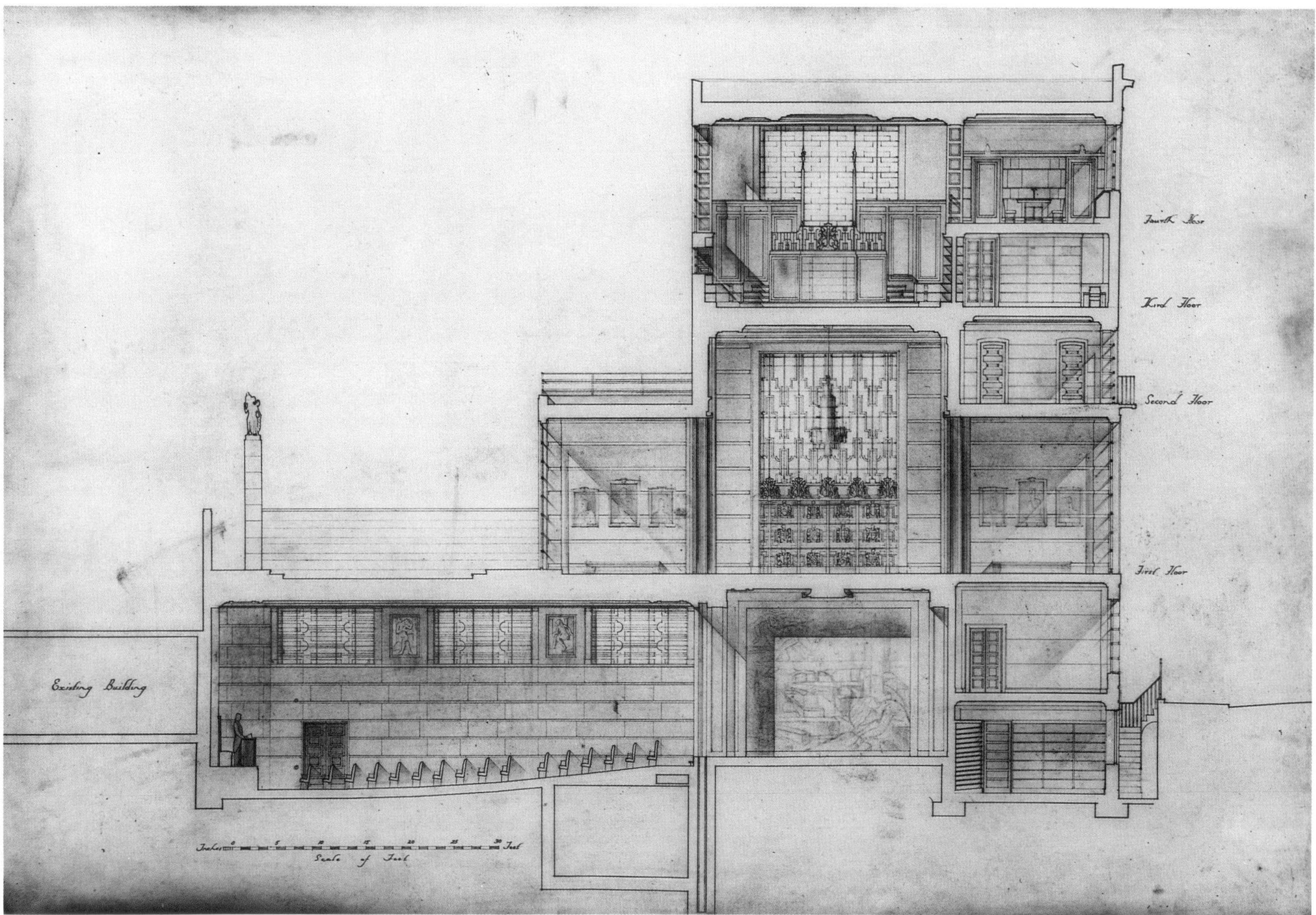

fig. 12 Section, design for the RIBA headquarters, 66 *Portland Place.* Grey Wornum, 1934. The British Architectural Library, RIBA.

fig. 13 The Brompton Boilers, installed with casts from the Architectural Museum. By courtesy of the Board of Trustees of the Victoria and Albert Museum, London.

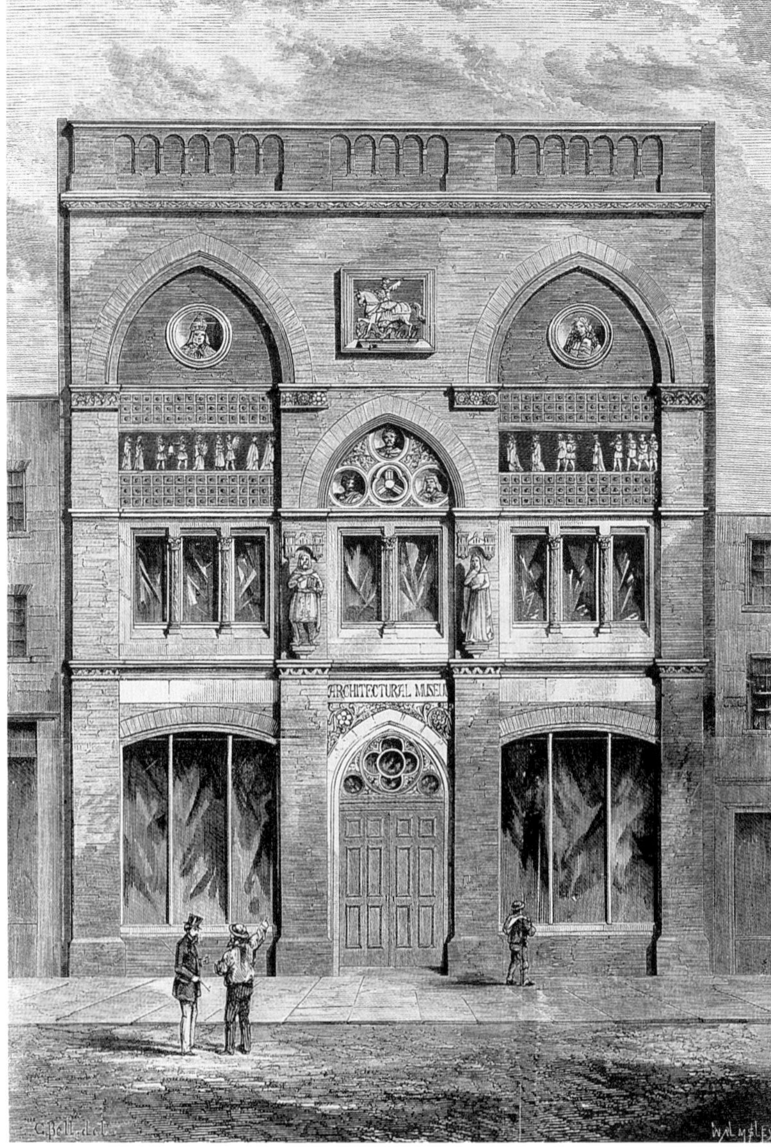

fig. 14 Façade of the Royal Architectural Museum. Engraving: Walmsley, drawing: C. Bell. Reproduced from *The Builder*, 24 July 1869. The British Architectural Library, RIBA.

Wyatt's house in Conduit Street conforms to the Helsinki, Stockholm, and Wroclaw type of architectural repository.

One other "museum" needs to be described. In 1825, Lewis Nockalls Cottingham, an architect and surveyor, built himself a house in Waterloo Road, London, to which he added specially designed accommodations for his large collection of medieval woodwork, Gothic carvings, and casts.[29] He could hardly have been unaware of the musée des Monuments français, and his collection was meant to educate craftsmen. Following his death in 1847, a *Descriptive Memoir* was published in 1850 for the sale by auction of the contents of what was then described as his Museum of Medieval Art. From this collection evolved the foundation of the Architectural Museum (later called the Royal Architectural Museum) in 1851.[30] First housed in a "most quaint" cock loft in Cannon Row, Westminster, where John Ruskin "poured forth his most telling eloquence,"[31] the museum's activities were moved in 1855 to the Brompton Boilers, a cast iron building that from 1856 housed the first South Kensington Museum (fig. 13).[32] It was not a happy union, and the Architectural Museum, minus its larger fragments and casts, was reinstalled in 1869 in a purpose-built museum in Tufton Street, Westminster, designed in a Gothic style by George Somers Clarke and Ewan Christian (fig. 14).

This was quite an event, for the Architectural Museum can claim to be the first purpose-built museum of its kind in the world. It was not acquisitive, however, but educational, and in 1893 it amalgamated with the Westminster School of Art. It soon became redundant, and by 1903 it had merged with, and become the home of, the Architectural Association. This pairing lasted until 1906, when its vast collection of more than four thousand casts was given to the Victoria and Albert Museum.[33] The remarkable building on Tufton Street was demolished in 1935. Its beginnings as Cottingham's museum can be seen to have served the Gothic revival in the same way that Soane's musuem served the classical tradition.

In the history of architectural museums the Museum of Construction and Building Materials of the Victoria and Albert Museum features large, for this was one of the earliest practical and permanent exhibitions of all sorts of building materials and building art.[34] According to the museum's catalogue of 1862, it contained "samples of building stones and marbles; specimens of all the best cements and asphalts; examples of the numerous applications of ceramic manufacture to the purpose of construction, more especially in this country and in France; such as tiles for roofing and flooring of the newest and most approved form, and clays; bricks hollow, solid and moulded, of various sorts; examples of many ingenious applications of these materials which are made in France, such as lintels, jambs, exterior and interior cornices." The museum was a natural development from the Great Exhibition of 1851, and it is significant that Henry Cole was the administrator of both, although the museum was designed and supervised by Captain Henry Fowke. Although this museum (which was eventually dispersed) can be seen as an ancestor of the modern building centre, it was much more. Its promotion of contemporary design through the installation of whole rooms and ambiences to present the best of art craftsmanship had a contemporaneity that can hardly be matched by museums of modern design today.

If the 1979 International Confederation of Architectural Museums meeting in Helsinki is seen as a catalyst to a reformation to come, it is so because of a growing awareness then that increasingly complex relationships to the representation and presentation of cultural artifacts are changing the museum experience. Although the display of architecture had changed little since the eighteenth century (exhibitions of architecture still had to grapple with the problem of outside-in – one that was fixed by the limitations of the paper image, the model, the cast, and space), by the late 1970s new technologies and electronic media were beginning to pose difficult questions.

Paralleling these dilemmas are unanswered questions about why vital architectural museums did not evolve in the twentieth century when great museums of modern art were born. A case study could be made of the Museum of Modern Art (MOMA) in New York, founded in 1929 as a museum of painting. In 1932 Philip Johnson and Henry-Russell Hitchcock organized the catalytic International Style exhibition, which initiated what has become the longest continuous programme of architectural exhibitions (140 shows to date) in any institution. Mies van der Rohe: Villas and Country Houses, of 1981, was a reminder that in 1963 the museum acquired the Mies archive. However, MOMA has never seen itself as an architectural repository or a documentation centre. The crucial difference between modern painting and modern architecture was that, while paintings can hang on walls, architecture still had to be exposed, as in the International Style exhibition, using large mounted photographs. (Photography was the only addition since the time of the Cassas gallery, to the media of architectural display.)

The era of MOMA's founding also saw architectural endeavour displayed in special subject exhibitions: the Deutsche Werkbund exhibition at Stuttgart in 1927, the Stockholm exhibition in 1928, the Frankfort ICAM Congress and the pavilions at the Barcelona World exhibition in 1929. In fact, world exhibitions have always been the "open air" museums, albeit temporary, for architecture.

The Helsinki ICAM meeting addressed a wide range of issues related to the contemporary architectural museum; there were great divides on many of these. However, there emerged a consensus that almost every institution was being compelled to acquire the paper evidence of architects' endeavours. This was causing financial headaches, as well as conservation and storage problems. Indeed, it seemed that paper was becoming the great determinant.

Neither Cassas nor Cottingham had seen the need to collect paper documents other than framed drawings. Even Sir John Soane made no statement of policy about his collection of drawings, and he never intended it to grow, or at least made no provision for its growth. In the past, if museums of art acquired large collections of architectural, decorative, and theatre drawings, on the whole they did so fortuitously. The "old master drawings" orientation prevailed, seen in the *Cabinet de dessin* at the Louvre, or at the Albertina in Vienna. All this began to change after World War II; following the decease of the last generation of architects who used standard paper and techniques of drawing, there grew an awareness on the part of state and provincial archivists that paper evidence must be kept intact and not partially dispersed or destroyed. What the executors of Sir Edwin Lutyens did to his great archive in the late 1940s (hundreds of his conceptual sketches on graph paper were destroyed), or the Royal Institute of British Architects to the Burn-Anderson archive in the 1950s (the Burn-Anderson drawings were divided up and sent out to the care of County Record Offices) would probably be condemned now. Thus, the architectural institution today is confronted by the problem that in many cases it must conserve all the remains of an architect's office, not only the small and large drawings, but the correspondence, contract books, minutes of committee meetings, photographs, drawing instruments, models, and even furniture. It is a daunting task.

The problem of conserving the contents of the offices of architects in private practice has never been satisfactorily solved. For example, although the United States Library of Congress ought to be the repository for the paper history of the nation, paradoxically it does not acquire such private archives. In Great Britain the situation is improved by the legal obligation of County Record Offices to take architectural collections into care. One can say that space and the logistical problems of cataloguing an archive determines policy at an architectural institution. Every institution belonging to ICAM faces this problem, and all are aware that paper artifacts are the most sensitive and difficult to preserve.

* * *

Now film, video (including television), and computers have changed all this in a startling way. The time is not far off when architecture will be able to take advantage of discoveries in other sciences (see fig. 15). Already the way in which new technologies can realistically animate existing buildings or reproductions of buildings opens up far horizons. Up to now, suites of historic rooms in museums, or buildings in open-air museums have been static displays accompanied by documentation. This may all

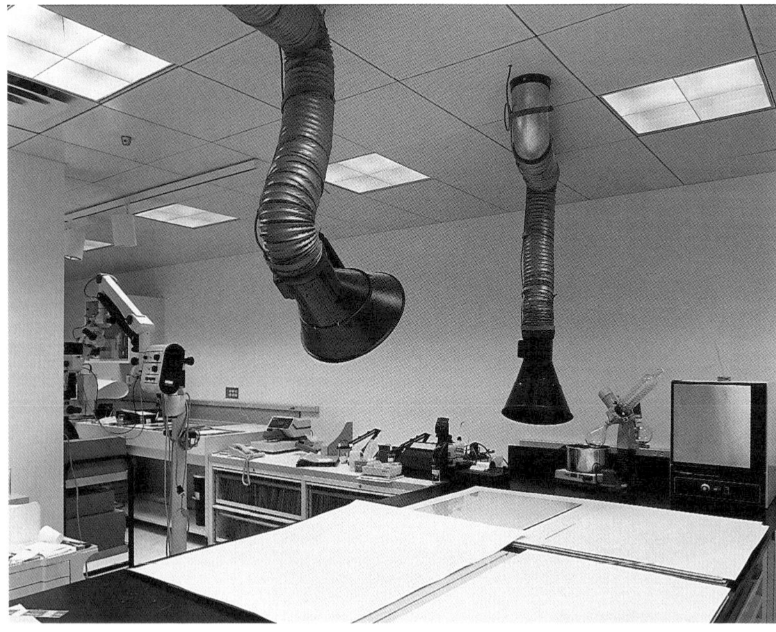

fig. 15 The CCA conservation laboratory. Photograph: Gabor Szilasi, 1988.

change. If by typing a coded number, facts can be sent across oceans, or if facsimile machines can deliver text in seconds, the age is not far off when images of drawings, or whole portable or paper museums, or even exhibitions, will be available from the exemplar banks of the second millennium.

These are all exciting developments that can be looked forward to in the future when architectural museums will be in instant communication with each other. However, these electronic means of reproduction and representation will never be a complete substitute for the real work of art on paper, because they cannot satisfy the scholar's need to sit at a study table to compare plan, elevation, and section in various permutations, or turn the pages of an illustrated architectural treatise; secondary reality will not subsume the primary reality. In the same sense there is no substitute for looking at the painting on the wall of an art musuem. Thus, little has changed since the paper museum of the seventeenth century, and in terms of the importance and pleasure of acquiring architectural knowledge, the scholar today is in the same situation as Cassiano dal Pozzo was in the renaissance.

1   There is no general history. I have been indebted to Werner Szambien's *Le Musée d'architecture* (Paris: Picard, 1988) on the architectural museum in France. I have benefitted from conversation with and advice from Barry Bergdoll, Phyllis Lambert, Larry Richards, and Barbara Shapiro, who have read my manuscript to advantage, and Professor Howard Burns, who has offered useful comment on the renaissance. I want to particularly thank Margaret Richardson, inspectress of Sir John Soane's Museum, for sharing with me her discoveries in Soane's archives.

2   The Cooper-Hewitt, founded in 1896 and based upon the musée des Arts décoratifs, was enriched by more than twelve thousand decorative, ornamental, architectural, and stage designs from the Piancastelli Collection. On the drawings collection of the Cooper-Hewitt, see John Harris, *Architectural Drawings in the Cooper-Hewitt Museum* (Washington, D.C.: Smithsonian Institute, 1982).

3   On sketchbooks, see Francis Haskell and Nicholas Penny, *Taste and the Antique* (New Haven: Yale University Press, 1981), 43ff.

4   There is dispute about the scale of acquisition by renaissance architects of the designs of others. However, there is no evidence that acquisition was other than partial. Giulio Romano possessed drawings by Raphael, and there is a scattering of miscellaneous drawings in the Palladio corpus, but no systematic collection appears to have been undertaken. Giorgio Vasari needs to be singled out, for clearly he matched his biographical collections with relevant drawings, but his was an exceptional situation.

5   Again there are reservations, for in 1614 Jones was not yet the British Vitruvius, but a celebrated masque-maker. For this acquisition see John Harris, *Inigo Jones and John Webb*, Catalogue of the Drawing Collection of the Royal Institute of British Architects, vol. 11 (Farnborough: Gregg International, 1972), and John Harris and Gordon Higgart, *The Architectural Drawings of Inigo Jones* (exhibition catalogue, New York: Drawings Centre, 1989).

6   I am grateful to Mr. Per Bjurström of the Nationalmuseum for information on the Tessins and for referring me to the printed catalogue of 1712.

7   Bjurström believes the drawings are the remains of the collection of the Office of Public Buildings, which was then housed in the royal palace. This supports what I have suspected: that France was plundered of drawings to enrich the exemplar bank.

8   There is still no history of the Talman Collection; but see John Harris, *William Talman: Maverick Architect* (London: Allen and Unwin, 1982). On Jones, see W.G. Keith, "Inigo Jones as a Collector," *RIBA Journal* 33 (19 Dec. 1925), 59ff; and John Harris, "Code Marks," in the typescript catalogue of the Burlington-Devonshire Collection (1960). See also John Harris, "John Talman's Design for his Wunderkammer," *Furniture History* 21 (1985): 211–14, figs. 2, 3.

9   We may also recollect Vasari's comment when he visited Guilio Romano and was taken to his *armadio* or cupboard, from which his drawings, and others, including some by Raphael, fell out. Vasari, *Lives*, ed. Gaston D.J. de Vere, 10 vols. (1913) 6: 166.

10   A history of the French *Works* is still lacking.

11   H.M. Colvin, ed., *The History of the King's Works, V, 1660–1782* (London: H.M. Stationary Office, 1976), 449.

12   First published by John Harris in *A Catalogue of British Drawings for Architecture, Decoration, Sculpture and Landscape Gardening 1550–1900 in American Collections* (Upper Saddle River, 1971), 322, plate 256. Figure 8 reproduces the perspective in the Metropolitan Museum of Art's

C.J. Richardson Album and is related to the plan and wall elevations in Sir John Soane's Museum, 43/10/13.

13   His design is illustrated in Thomas Madox, *Antiquus Dialogus* (1711), 63–64.

14   For the history of academies see N. Pevsner, *Academies of Art, Past and Present* (Cambridge: Cambridge University Press, 1940), a work that curiously ignores planning and operating functions, which Pevsner treats in detail in his *A History of Building Types* (London: Thames and Hudson, 1970).

15   On Somerset House see John Harris, *Sir William Chambers* (University Park: Pennsylvania State University Press, 1970), 96ff.

16   Information supplied by H.M. Colvin.

17   J. Mordaunt Crook, *The British Museum* (London: Allen Lane, 1972); see Pevsner, *A History of Building Types*, 111 ff., for the history of museums; for the designs, see plates 14 and 15.

18   All over Europe the older academies must have possessed accumulations of architectural artifacts: framed drawings, models, possibly even models of towns such as those of the Musée des plans et reliefs in Paris; and the engineering schools would have had models of bridges. In other words, these academies – and one can single out Jacques-François Blondel's École des arts in Paris, or his son Georges-François Blondel's School of Design in Covent Garden – were already taking on the character of museums, albeit probably muddled in the manner of display. See Georges-François Blondel, *Description of an Exhibition, Which the Sieur Blondel, … Intends to Give to the Public of His Works, at His House under the Piazzas next to King Street, Covent Garden* (London: C. Clarke, 1772).

19   For this part of my history I am indebted to Werner Szambien's "Les Origines du Musée d'Architecture en France" in *Gazette des Beaux-Arts* 108 (October 1986): 135–140, and have now benefitted from his *Le Musée d'Architecture*, as well as from Barry Bergdoll's percipient comments.

20   On Chichi, see Anita Buttner, *Korkmodelle von Antonia Chichi* (exhibition catalogue, Kassel: Staatlichen Kunstsammlungen Kassel, no. 6 [n.d.]).

21   For models, see also D. Poulet, "Architectural Models: The Birth of a Museum of Architecture in France during the Revolution," *Lotus International* 35 (1982): 32–35; and, for an account of Fouquet, see Werner Szambien, *Jean-Nicolas-Louis Durand* (Paris: Picard, 1984), 160, sec. 18.

22   Pointed out by Margaret Richardson, inspectress of the museum, who is working on a history of the museum and of Soane as a collector.

23   Soane's Museum, PSA 33.

24   See the current *New Description* of Sir John Soane's Museum (1986); see also Sir John Summerson, "The Soane Museum, 13 Lincoln's Inn Fields" in *John Soane Architectural Monographs* (London: Academy Edition, 1983); and John Britton, *Union of Architecture, Sculpture and Painting Exemplified by a Series of Illustrations with Descriptive Accounts of the House and Galleries of John Soane* (London, 1827). Margaret Richardson explained the relevant drawings to me.

25   See Soane's Museum 32/2A,11 of 23 July 1792. Here Soane proposes a table six feet eight inches by four feet (203 x 122 cm), a wainscot desk three feet five inches wide (104 cm), a "deal case" three feet nine inches by two feet seven inches (114 x 79 cm), and a recess inscribed for "Presses for drawing," perhaps shelves. See also PSA 33 of 20 July 1808, and PSA 15, showing a plan chest. It is significant that John Britton, in *Illustrations of the Public Buildings of London*, 2 vols. (London: J. Taylor, 1825–27, 1: 318), describes the hanging wall storage as "novel in design," commenting that in a

room just seventeen by thirteen by eleven feet (518 x 396 x 336 cm) it
provided 1,656 square feet (154 m^2) of storage. In 1819 Thomas Hope had
installed a form of hanging-picture storage in his Picture Gallery at Duchess
Street.

26 See *New Description*, and in particular the "Chronology of Sir John Soane's
Museum" in appendix 1, 56–62.

27 For a general account of the rise of the profession, including the European
context, see William H. White, *Architecture and Public Buildings: Their Relation
To School, Academy, and State* (London: P.S. King, 1884); and for the
profession in Britain see J.A. Gotch, ed., *The Growth and Work of the Royal
Institute of British Architects, 1834–1934* (London: RIBA, 1934); and Frank
Jenkins, *Architect and Patron* (Oxford: Oxford University Press, 1961),
chapter six. Barry Bergdoll has pointed out that A.T.L. Vaudoyer and others
had proposed a society of architects in 1806.

28 *Catalogue of the Drawings Collection*, vol. 5 (1973). Exeter Hall was designed
by J. Gandy-Deering in 1830–31; the room as shown by Moore was
presumably purpose-built for the Architectural Society.

29 On Cottingham, about whom little has been written, see H. M. Colvin,
Biographical Dictionary of British Architects 1600–1840 (Cambridge: Harvard
University Press, 1978), 234–45; *The Builder* 5 (1847): 502; and also L.N.
Cottingham, *Descriptive Memoir* (London, 1850).

30 On the Architectural Museum, see Sir John Summerson, *The Architectural
Association, 1847–1947* (London: Pleiades, 1947); and Peter Wylde, "The
First Exhibition: The Architectural Association and the Royal Architectural
Museum," *Architectural Association Annual Review* (1981).

31 Sir George Gilbert Scott, *Personal Recollections*, qtd. in White, *Architecture and
Public Buildings*, 2.

32 For the early history of this South Kensington site, see John Physick, *The
Victoria and Albert Museum: The History of the Building* (Oxford: Phaidon,
1982); for the Brompton Boilers, also see Physick, 9–12.

33 In 1876 the *Catalogue of the Collections of the Royal Architectural Museum* listed
the casts and provided a descriptive account of educational policy.

34 Physick, *The Victoria and Albert Museum*.

Portfolio 1

Photographs by Clara Gutsche,
David Miller, and Laura Volkerding
September 1985 – September 1988

Trenton limestone block at carrières Saint-Marc, Saint-Marc-des-Carrières, Quebec. Photograph: Laura Volkerding, September 1987.

The Shaughnessy House at the start of construction. Photograph: David Miller, November 1985.

The construction site after completion of second vault floor. Photograph: David Miller, September 1985.

Auditorium wing of the new building and the Shaughnessy House conservatory. Photograph: David Miller, January 1987.

The partially constructed north elevation, new building. Photograph: David Miller, January 1987.

Bay window in the drawing room, Shaughnessy House. Photograph: Clara Gutsche,
February 1987.

Staircase, Shaughessy House. Photograph: Clara Gutsche, February 1987.

307·VII

The wood frame for a Serlian dormer window, Shaughnessy House. Photograph: Clara Gutsche, April 1987.

Reception and dining rooms looking toward the entrance hall, Shaughnessy House. Photograph: Clara Gutsche, February 1987.

View through Tearoom to conservatory, Shaughnessy House. Photograph: Clara Gutsche, February 1987.

Ductwork adjacent to the octagonal gallery, new building. Photograph: Clara Gutsche, June 1987.

Mechanical room on second vault level, new building. Photograph: Clara Gutsche, April 1987.

The Scholars' Wing, new building.
Photograph: Clara Gutsche,
January 1987.

View of the main galleries from across the Entrance Court, new building. Photograph:
Clara Gutsche, June 1987.

Mock-up of one of the square galleries, new building. Photograph: Clara Gutsche,
March 1988.

Partially constructed storage racks in the photographs collection vault, new building. Photograph: Clara Gutsche, January 1988.

The prints and drawings collection vault, new building. Photograph: Clara Gutsche, August 1987.

The north elevation of the new building, showing partially completed cornice. Photograph: David Miller, September 1988.

The Entrance Court, new building. Photograph: David Miller, June 1988.

View through the Shaughnessy House conservatory toward the auditorium wing. Photograph: Laura Volkerding, September 1987.

Design Imperatives

PHYLLIS LAMBERT

Developing a Programme and an Institution

From the beginning, a building designed specifically to house
the Centre Canadien d'Architecture / Canadian Centre for
Architecture (CCA) was integral to the concept of establishing an
architectural museum and study centre. The most basic need was
to provide a place that was large enough and secure enough to
store the growing collection and to make its holdings accessible to
researchers and known to the public. Identity of place is essential
for an institution whose mission is to engage the public in discourse. Since there was no model for such an institution there was
no precedent for such a building. The CCA had to be invented.
This essay traces the interrelationship between design and
programme, clarifies the purposes of the new institution, and
brings into focus the issues that – as founder and director of the
CCA – I judged to be imperatives of design which informed the
development of the CCA.

In 1980, its first year, the CCA worked principally out of my
architectural office in Montréal. The drawings collection was
housed there, a very small library staff acquired books (which
were stored off-site), and a curator and an assistant acquired and
accessioned the growing photographs collection, which was
housed in New York City. But plans for staff and collections
development indicated the need for larger quarters.

Two sets of preliminary plans preceded the present design of the
building. The first plans, developed in late 1980–81, were for

temporary quarters in a downtown Montréal warehouse; a freestanding, four-story, reinforced concrete structure where the collections would not be exposed to possible fire or water damage from adjacent spaces. Here the CCA would be able to shelve the library collection in order to begin cataloguing. Similarly, conservation and cataloguing could begin for the prints and drawings collection, and eventually for the archives.

Plans to prepare the warehouse building for use by the CCA eventually went far beyond a renovation scheme, to include developing a programme for a fully functioning museum. It became clear, however, that the warehouse building would have been too small for this purpose. It would not have accommodated long-term growth; moreover, because of the restricted floor-size (thirty metres square) it would have been necessary to separate the collections by floor, with exhibitions on the ground floor (fig. 16). This scheme would have given exhibitions an unwanted primacy, since visitors would have been able to see an exhibition without being aware of the other functions of the CCA, such as the library and the study centre. Even public access to facilities such as a bookstore and restaurant would have posed a problem.

But – most important – the arrangement of collections by floor would have been inappropriate for a centre which was intellectually structured around the interrelationships of the different sources for the study of architecture. In this way the process of design itself clarified operating goals and procedures. The CCA required a place in which books, drawings, photographs, manuscripts, letters, and account books could be looked at together. Located on separate floors, the collection could not be perceived as a whole.

The block that had been occupied only by the Shaughnessy House since the demolition in 1972 of neighbouring buildings had the desired characteristics. With an area of 1.2 hectares – twelve times the ground area of the warehouse site – it could accommodate large floor areas.

A new programme to define the relationships of those who would use the building was elaborated. It was most important that on entering, visitors understand the place, and researchers be aware of public programmes. Operationally, it was essential that each

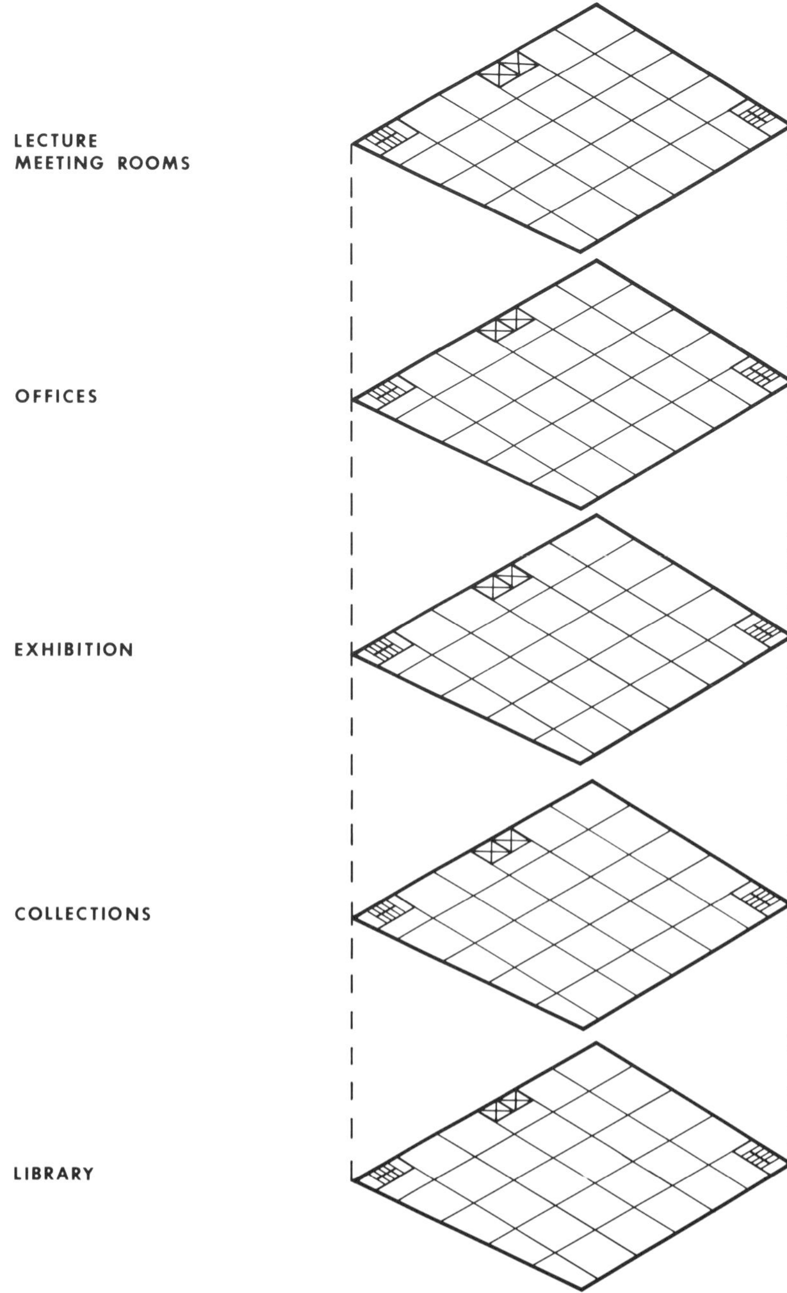

fig. 16 Schematic plan for temporary housing of the CCA in a former Hudson's Bay warehouse. Office of Phyllis Lambert, architect, 1980.

department be informed about the holdings and acquisitions of the others, and that the curators and cataloguers of each collection be in constant contact with each other. Exhibition and library spaces had to be firmly linked, and all curatorial functions closely related spatially. The new programme called for some collection vaults to be located on the same level as the curatorial offices, with a secondary storage level below. The whole was to be underground; later, with expansion, this below-ground space would be transformed to collection storage, and programme areas would be developed in two wings above ground (see figs. 42–49).

The underground scheme was rejected for practical and conceptual reasons. As the CCA developed, it became evident that early projections of the space required had been quite inadequate. While in 1980 the programme for the warehouse scheme had called for 6,875 square metres of space and a staff of 36, by the end of 1983 the CCA already occupied 3,344 square metres in downtown office buildings in Montréal and had a staff of 50. These rented quarters did not allow for public programmes or expansion; they were dedicated to curatorial and administrative functions and to the shelving and inventorying of collections. The underground scheme did not provide sufficient space for future expansion.[1]

It was also problematic in other ways. Its generating idea was that of reestablishing the Shaughnessy House as a villa, surrounded – as a villa should be – by gardens. A series of pergolas would serve two functions: to define the edges of a park, and to perform as light wells for the undergound exhibition galleries, curatorial offices, and workrooms. But this idea of the Shaughnessy House as a place of reception was compromised by the extensive space needed for the entry sequence. Half of the house would have been a passage, a route from the exterior to other rooms in the house and to the underground museum. Moreover, historically, the Shaughnessy House was not a villa, built in open countryside, but a double house presented as a mansion set within spacious landscaped grounds. There had been similar properties adjacent and across the street. It became clear that the Shaughnessy House alone, without additional buildings on the block, did not have the incidence, mass, and scale necessary to continue the definition of the street as a boulevard. Alone on a 1.2-hectare site, it could not provide the urban context needed to reconstruct a demolished, highway-scarred area sprinkled with highrise buildings.[2]

The underground scheme was a turning point. Its conceptual basis was the unity of the collections; its strategy was one of universal space – a historical solution whose architectural possibilities were still being explored, a century after its invention, for railway stations and exposition halls.[3] According to this scheme, the library reading room and the exhibition room were initially conceived of as one large space divided by a transparent wall. A carefully worked out concrete waffle slab ceiling was to be supported by columns spaced on twelve-metre centres in two directions. The structure was the architecture, and its material – concrete – was symbolic of being underground, representing the earth and rock substrata. During the winter of 1983, I sketched many schemes for defining these spaces as a library and an exhibition hall. It became clear to me that the difficulty of finding a satifactory architectural solution lay in the basic definition of the problem. Why impose and expose an industrial structural system for functions requiring spaces as different in scale and quality as curatorial offices, stacks, library reading rooms, and exhibition galleries?

The experience of the CCA's first exhibition, "Photography and Architecture," was critical to this realization. Between September 1982 and October 1983 the exhibition was shown at three venues: as part of the Photokina in Cologne, at the Art Institute of Chicago, and at the Cooper-Hewitt Museum in New York.[4] The best installation was unquestionably the one at the Cooper-Hewitt, where the photographs were presented in suites of architecturally articulated rooms in the house that was formerly the Carnegie Mansion. In these spaces, appropriate and telling relationships could be established between daguerreotypes in small, elegant, velvet-lined wall cases; framed photographs on the walls; and large albums displayed sculpturally and dramatically in freestanding cases. The temporary arrangements of modular walls used at the other venues were not conducive to the viewing of relatively small works of art on paper.

At this point it became necessary to review the premises and design process. The first step was to relocate the design process to Montréal. The next task was to choose an architect. One possibility was to hold an architectural competition, which might have been particularly appropriate to an institution that is itself concerned with architecture. I have been asked why I did not choose this option for the CCA building. The are many reasons, but mostly, as an architect myself, I wished to direct the building programme along with the development of the institution. After working on the first scheme with an office a few hours away in Toronto and subsequently with my own office even farther away in Los Angeles, I wished to have a much more constant relationship to design development. I did not want to be only the client, but to work closely with the architect.

It was important to me that the architect of the building deeply understand the architecture of Montréal. My commitment to Montréal was that of an expatriate of over twenty-five years who now saw the city with new understanding. The years from 1944 to 1971 – when I was at university and later, training to be an architect – encompassed a time of dramatic urban change and witnessed the decomposition of the traditional city.

In 1970, Montréal was a rare example of a large North American city whose structure had not suffered dramatically in those years. It was an ideal laboratory in which to study and analyze a city which is still composed of neighbourhoods, through whose buildings could be read a long and specific history. The neighbourhoods – spatially and temporally – tell the story of the city's development: through the grouping of building types; and the relationships of building materials to building type, buildings to street, street to neighbourhood, and neighbourhood to city. This clear a text can be read in very few major North American cities. In Montréal, urban form and architectural language express the cultural history of a city which was originally French, then dominated by the British, then again French-speaking and cosmopolitan.

Montréal does not deliver its secrets easily. Its urban and architectural history were unknown in 1971 when I began (with Richard Pare) a photographic mission to study the greystone buildings of Montréal as a means of understanding the urban character of the city. At the same time, I established a research group that led to the formation at the CCA of the Documentation Centre on the Architecture of Montréal.[5] The photographic and archival documentation led to my involvement in architectural and urban conservation, and laid the basis for the establishment of the CCA.

Had I not found an architect who was looking intelligently and sensitively at the city and its buildings, would there have been a competition? The question will never be answered. Peter Rose had returned to Montréal from architectural school at Yale University at about the same time that I had returned from Chicago. For him, as for me, Montréal was a subject of study, a treatise on how buildings are put together and how they relate to each other. Although we had been trained very differently (he by Charles Moore, I by Mies van der Rohe), the architecture of Montréal was our common ground. Over a number of years we met, tentatively at first, to discuss architecture (he worked as a consultant on the CCA warehouse project). In September 1983 we began to meet intensively to discuss the design of the CCA building. In October 1983 he began preliminary design; construction began in June 1985.

Issues of Design

At both the École des Beaux-Arts in Paris and at Mies van der Rohe's school of architecture at the Illinois Institute of Technology (IIT), Vitruvian principles of architecture held sway. Under the systems of training at both schools, students were asked to design a generic building for an undefined or idealized site. In the one case the architectural solutions were developed from the taxis of classical architecture, in the other they were to develop from the investigation of new rules a taxis for building with industrial materials. In both cases context was not important. Today, after extensive destruction in war and "peace" of the central areas of North American and European cities, the relationship of buildings to their urban context demands our closest attention. In its design, the CCA building is both siteless – concerned with the taxis of building; with commodity, firmness, and beauty – and deeply embedded in its site and in the building traditions of Montréal.

The Siteless Building

Certain design issues that were independent of site, such as order, light, and procession, preoccupied Peter and myself. The sense of order in architecture is hierarchical, involving – among other things – rank, position, the classical orders. It implies the ordering of parts, the relationships of part to whole, and it is based on a sense of the propriety of these relationships. In the CCA building, these relationships are evident in plan and section, as they are in the exterior and interior elevations.

One of the greatest challenges of the design was to create an architectural order without an apparent structural expression. Mies's buildings provided some clues – in the steel skin that represents the underlying structure and the brick wall planes that subsume structure in his IIT campus, and in the free wall planes of his studies for courthouses and museums. Inside the CCA building, columns at the centre line and the point of juncture between the new and the old buildings proclaim the presence of the underlying skeleton, which is otherwise alluded to through the ordering of openings (doors, windows, and skylights), expansion joints, the connections of metal railings, and even the placement of air diffuser grills and the hardware of security systems. Through a skillfully expressed hierarchy of windows and the coursing and rustication of stone, Peter has implied the weave of structure in the exterior walls. The same ordering is found in the use of metal throughout the building.

Light and procession were discussed from the beginning, and Peter and I determined that they would have a primary role in design. We were both very interested in the use of natural light to modulate the perception of space and in the way the size and location of light apertures can direct and qualify movement through a building. The use of daylight in exhibition galleries was a particular problem. Natural light, which had in mid-century been excluded from exhibition spaces by conservators and curators, was beginning to be reintroduced in gallery design, but not in spaces for the display of works on paper. The chemical composition of paper and the light-sensitive nature of media applied to it – such as watercolour, ink, and silver salts – cause prints, drawings, and photographs to deteriorate when subjected to intense illumination over a period of time. This was an important consideration since the CCA collection is almost wholly composed of works of art on paper. However, the alienating environment of a "black box" was not acceptable either.

The solution to the problem of admitting natural light while protecting the objects was developed through an approach which was natural to Peter – that of defining the true nature of the task. The two functions had to be separated. Only controllable artificial light would be used to illuminate the objects, a standard practice. However, a baroque play of natural light could be introduced through lanterns in the vaulted ceilings of the galleries. This ceiling design allows the effects of changes in the sun's position or of a cloud briefly veiling the sun to be perceived and yet not to affect the allowable light level on the works exhibited. But in the reading rooms, where works would not be continuously exposed, a much higher level of illumination was possible and desirable. These rooms could be suffused with daylight.

In our design discussions, through models and drawings, principles and positions were clarified and refined. Throughout this process our greatest pleasure was learning how to identify structure and non-structure, to define the roles of the parts – their relationship to each other and to the whole – without making a structuralist building.

Although the initial concept came together rather quickly, designing the building took much longer than anticipated because the process was much more complicated than we had imagined. There were effectively many buildings: the "laboratory building," including the vaults; the "office building"; the "public building," itself composed of six or seven different types of spaces; and the renovated building. Each required extensive research. Although it was known that standards of environmental control were critical for works of art on paper, in the early 1980s there was no clear agreement about what these should be for each medium. We had not even imagined the complexity of the electronic controls needed to monitor environmental conditions in the building. The same was true for control over access to the collection, over security, fire protection, and communication nodes for computer access throughout the building.

Once the special architectural problems were defined, they were discussed among the wider community of the CCA staff, the project engineers, and the security, communications, lighting, and landscape consultants. All the materials: floor coverings, paints, and cleaning solvents to be used in the vaults were subjected to chemical analysis by the CCA head of conservation. Peter worked with collections heads and staff and reviewed conclusions with me. Throughout, Peter and I met every week. We looked at drawings, we looked at models, we talked excitedly and calmly, we drew, we argued. Just the two of us.

The restoration of the Shaughnessy House, supervised by Denis St-Louis, involved a different kind of work. It required specialized knowledge of restoration and the interventions required to adapt to new or elaborated functions – such as reinforcing the structure to carry office loads, adding skylights, and installing new kitchens.

The principles of design which applied to restoration also related to those of the new building: coding what was the original fabric and what was replaced was equivalent to distinguishing between what was structural and what was not. Restoration, however, is very different from building. New construction is additive – a transformation of the diagrammatic to the complex, ever changing in scale, surface, and colour. The process may be compared to a film about Picasso creating a painting: at every stage one wants to say, "stop!" but relentlessly the work goes on. Restoration, on the other hand, is almost a surgical intervention: like Vesalius's anatomical engravings, uncovering layers of skin, tissue, threads of energy, finally laying bare the structure through successive stages of uncovering and recovering, subtraction and renewal.

Moreover, major restoration work is artisanal rather than industrial. The mahogany panelling of the Shaughnessy House (including the ceiling of the Tearoom), the bannisters, the panelled doors, the wooden shutters, the Corinthian Ananassa columns of the salon, and the decorative motifs were transported from Montréal to workshops downriver at Deschambault, Portneuf, Saint-Jean-Port-Joli. These woodworking shops divided the slow, specialized work of refinishing, strengthening, and replacing parts that had been vandalized. Their sylvan setting above the river and the attitudes of the skilled woodcarvers who live and work there belong to the worlds of Thomas Hardy and the medieval building associations of France – the *compagnons.* They contrast sharply with the hierarchically organized, industrialized workshops of contemporary construction.

The Sited Building

From the outset Peter and I wanted to make a building that was related to the history and culture of the city. A major role of the new building and its surrounding land was to reknit the urban tissue of an area made derelict by highway construction in the 1960s. The building had to – as any work of architecture must – add to and heighten the architectural quality of its neighbourhood, at the same time reaching beyond to encompass not only the best traditions of the city but also the timeless values of architecture, the poetics of order.

The architecture of Montréal is a construct of the seventeenth-century French mind. Three powerful aspects of the mentality of its founders still mark the city today: *seigneurial* governance, a rational geometric order imposed on the land to structure settlement, and a carefully prescribed manner of building. By rights granted to the Sulpician Seminary under an ancient French system of feudal prerogatives, the Gentlemen of the Séminaire de Saint-Sulpice became the *seigneurs* as well as the priests of the island of Montréal in 1677. As landlords of the island, the Sulpicians had the obligation to settle the land, which they organized through land grants. The concessions granted by the Sulpicians on the island of Montréal were an orderly series of long, narrow strips of land starting at the St. Lawrence River, and running northward inland and perpendicular to the river (fig. 17). The concessions were modular, either two *arpents* wide by fifteen *arpents* in length (approximately one hundred by eight hundred metres) or one *arpent* by thirty (approximately fifty metres by one-and-a-half kilometres). As settlement advanced, these modules were extended northward (fig. 18). The long north–south streets of modern-day Montréal, which run between the river and Mount Royal, were laid out along or within the cadastral lines of these seventeenth-century concessions (see page 148). Streets running east–west were essentially circumstantial, following geomorphological features.

Among colonial cities it is unusual for an original pattern of settlement to extend over such a large area. In Montréal, the seventeenth-century cadastral system was so deeply embedded in the nineteenth-century city that it directed its development and future growth into the twentieth century. In developing the design of the CCA building and its gardens, Peter and I were intent on embodying and signifying the cadastral division as it has ordered

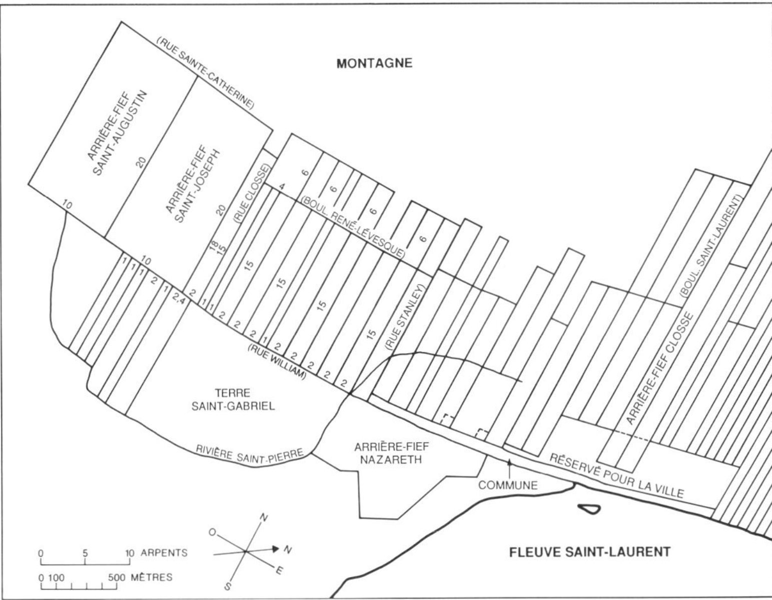

fig. 17 Farm concessions in Montreal in 1663. Research: Alan Stewart, cartography: Daniel Thibault, 1988 (adapted from Marcel Trudel, *Montréal, la formation d'une société 1642–1663*, 1976). CCA (AR1988:0011).

the urban structure of Montréal. The Shaughnessy House was built as a double house, each house a mirror image of the other. The pronounced quoigning at the centre line of the building marks the original cadastral subdivision between the two properties. The line is expressed on the interior by a sequence of columns between the old and the new buildings (see page 82). On the exterior it is marked by a centre cut, an expansion joint on the entrance face. Similarly, the cadastral lines that defined the earlier properties immediately to the east and west of the house are signified by the centre lines of the Entrance Court and the Library Court of the new building. Beyond, to the north and south, they are also the primary lines of organization for the CCA Garden and Baile Park, giving expression to the land forms and architecture of the city as an archaeology continually discovered.

As we worked, identifying these elements strengthened for us principles of urban and architectural design – most importantly, the principle of starting with what exists and picking up the clues offered by the city and its buildings, clues that history, when understood, provides.

The relationship of the building's footprint to the corpus of institutional buildings in the city, the figural E composed of pavilions and wings, was embedded in all designs for the building on this site, in the composition formed by the new and existing buildings. Finally, the material of revetment, grey limestone, is also an important element of connection to Montréal's architecture.

fig. 18 St. Andrew ward, 1912. Reproduced from Charles Edward Goad, *Atlas, City of Montreal and Vicinity*, 1912–14.
The Shaughnessy House is on cadastral lot number 1630.

The Manner of Building

If Montréal had not been settled initially by the French, its buildings would have been of brick, as were the representative buildings of the British colonies and of the United Empire Loyalists who came to Canada. Brick was the building material of the British, stone of the French. The first brick contract for a building exterior known in Montréal called for a stone building to be faced with brick.[6] Thirteen of the fifteen owners of brick houses mentioned in building contracts from the period 1800 to 1830 in Montréal were from either Great Britain or the United States.

The art of masonry is the core of French architecture. For the architect and writer Mathurin Jousse, writing in 1635, it was the "secret of architecture"; for the historian Pérouse de Montclos, writing in 1982, it was the essence of "*l'architecture à la française.*"[7] It is not surprising, therefore, to find Montréal – then the second largest French city in the world – recorded in the 1911 census of Canada as the city with the country's greatest concentration of stone buildings. Today, greystone buildings continue to form a network across the island of Montréal. The unity and structural clarity they give to the city is unique on this continent.

All Montréal's quarries are located in the two limestone formations, Chazy and Trenton, which underlie the island. At the edge of the Precambrian shield of northern Quebec a great inundation of the seas laid down the Montréal limestones. These fossil-laden formations are evidence of an extinct life that settled on the ocean floor five hundred million years ago. The Trenton formation underlies the greater part of Montréal island. It runs in the bed of the St. Lawrence River along its north shore to Quebec City.

Because of weathering and differences of chemical composition, slight differences in the colour of limestone develop. The presence of iron oxides produces cream-coloured to brown and reddish stones. Greys, blues, and blacks are due to finely divided carbonaceous matter. The colour of the Trenton formation is also a dark brown or a brownish grey.

The stone of the CCA building is a light grey-brown, richly figured Trenton. A Swedish naturalist, Pehr Kalm, who visited the area in 1749, wrote that the limestones of the region consist of "a compact calcarous-stone, mixed with grains of spar, of the same colour, it is full of petrified striated shells of pectinites."[8] The stone of the CCA comes from the only quarry now producing limestone for building purposes in the Montréal region. The quarry, at Saint-Marc-des-Carrières, lies on the north shore of the St. Lawrence River, halfway between Montréal and Quebec City. Peter Rose and I went there to learn how stone is quarried, cut, and finished. I was familiar with local requirements and practices from inspection of eighteenth- and nineteenth-century buildings and their specifications and contracts. However, practices changed in the first decades of the twentieth century with the introduction of huge carborundum saw-blades twenty feet in diameter, and the use of power tools for finishing the stone.

Observation of twentieth-century limestone revetment in Montréal shows a casual attitude toward the exigencies of the material. Stone was cut and laid randomly, some pieces with the grain laid horizontally in their bed, others vertically, others with a cross-cut grain, or diagonally. This mêlée is the result of the application: stones veneered, bearing no weight. However, even in the last quarter of the nineteenth century, bearing stone was laid vertically, and the resulting disintegration and spalling could be seen in many of the stones of the Shaughnessy House before they were recently refaced.

We sought to make the CCA well built and respectful of the best construction traditions. The Montréal climate required a thick outer wall, a cushioned envelope to neutralize the extremes of temperature. The stone facing, four and six inches thick, is self-supporting, bearing its own weight up to the topmost stones, which are pinned in place. The cut and bedding of the stone is symbolic of the forces. In the areas of greatest stress, on the lintels and along the string courses, the stone is laid in its bed. The rest of the stone – whether the rusticated base courses, or the ashlar of the body of the building – is cut against the grain, minimizing weathering and at the same time emphasizing the figure of the stone.

Some aspects of the articulation of the stone of the CCA are found in nineteenth-century buildings throughout the city. For example, a masonry tradition of great interest, which is no longer evident, is the stepping back of the stone at each floor. In eighteenth-century building specifications this diminution of the thickness of the wall, as it rose, was referred to as a wall "in its fruit."[9] The set back planes of the CCA walls are more than a technique, they are, primarily, a formal gesture.

The Landscape

The river and the mountain – the St. Lawrence and Mount Royal – are the iconic elements of Montréal and the original sites of fortification and settlement. The one presaged a city of commerce, the other an earthly paradise, a *paradis terrestre,* of orchards and farms, of villas and mansions.

The CCA stands on the edge of the *paradis terrestre,* originally the Sulpician Domain.[10] This section of Montréal parallels the old city in historic importance. Here, the first stone fortification was built by 1694 as a mission to christianize the Iroquois and the Huron. Two of its stone towers remain three blocks north of the CCA site (see fig. 62). (The stone walls of the Fort de la montagne significantly pre-date the use of stone to replace the wooden palisade which surrounded the city. The stone fortifications of the city were begun in 1717 and completed in 1737.) At the end of the seventeenth century it was already changing from fortified mission to villa, a *maison de plaisance,* in keeping with the tastes of Vachon de Belmont, the aristrocratic Sulpician who built the fort, and with those of the Gentlemen of Saint-Sulpice in France.[11]

The original pastoral character of the area is known from iconographic and textual sources. Drawings and descriptions of the seventeenth and eighteenth centuries show vineyards, orchards, and gardens, as well as dovecotes, vast breeding grounds for fowl, and pasturage. Quite properly for his time – the end of the eighteenth century – Isaac Weld emphasized the picturesque in his description:

The base of this mountain is surrounded with neat country houses and gardens, and partial improvements have been made about one-third of the way up; the remainder is entirely covered with lofty trees. On that side towards the river is a large old monastery, with extensive enclosures walled in, round which the garden has been cleared for some distance. This open part is covered with a rich verdure; and the woods encircling it, instead of being over-run with brushwood, are quite clear at bottom, so that you may here roam about at pleasure for miles together, shaded by the lofty trees from the rays of the sun.

The view from hence is grand beyond description. A prodigious expanse of country is laid open to the eye, with the noble river St. Lawrence winding through it, which may be traced from the remotest part of the horizon. The river comes from the right, and flows smoothly on, after passing down the tremendous rapids above the town, where it is hurried over huge rocks and with a noise that is heard even up the mountain. On the left below you appears the town of Montreal, with its churches, monasteries, glittering spires and the shipping under its old walls.[12]

The traditions of the Sulpicians were continued in the eighteenth and early nineteenth centuries with the construction of private villas and mansions in the area, and the relocation to the area of three of the four founding institutions of Montréal, which moved from the old city in the middle of the nineteenth century. These three buildings are the work of the greatest Montréal architects of their times: the Grand Séminaire (1857) and the Collège de Montréal (1870) of John Ostell (the first trained architect to settle in Montréal) and his successor Maurice Perrault; the Maison-mère des Soeurs Grises (1869–80) of Victor Bourgeau; and the Maison-mère de la Congrégation de Notre-Dame (1905–08) of Jean-Omer Marchand, the first Canadian architect to be trained at the École des Beaux-Arts.

In contrast, the Sulpician Domain known as Terre Saint-Gabriel, on the plain below what is now boulevard René-Lévesque, was used for pasturage and then warehousing. The construction of the Lachine Canal in the 1820s and its improvement in the 1840s supported the development "below the hill" of industry and working-class housing.[13] This sharp contrast between land uses on the upside and downside domains is still evident in the CCA sites north and south of the boulevard, and is reflected in the CCA Garden.

The CCA landscape was designed by Diana Gerrard and Gunta Mackars, Peter Rose, and myself. Its principal elements are Baile Park, at the entrance of the CCA, and the CCA Garden, designed principally by Melvin Charney. The land on which the park and the gardens were to be created had been derelict land, laid waste by highway construction three decades ago.[14] The new landscape had to fulfill several roles. It had to delight and it had to heal the scars of traffic engineering. It was also appropriate that the new park and garden of the CCA relate to the ecological and built history of site and city and comment on urban landscape, a subject sorely neglected in Montréal today.

The new building and the Shaughnessy House occupy one third of a 1.2-hectare block. The remaining two thirds have been landscaped to form Baile Park, a forecourt comprising just under ½ hectare.[15] Two small courtyards – the Visitors' Court and the Scholars' Court – are encompassed within the envelope of the building.

The structure of this landscape is extended to the south, across boulevard René-Lévesque, by a sculpture garden of ⅔ hectare. It continues the CCA's domain to the edge of the escarpment, where the land drops sharply to the railway and highway below. The entry and exit to the highway bind the east and west edges of both the gardens and the city block that holds the building. Situated as it is at a major access point to downtown Montréal, the garden heralds entry to the city. Both Baile Park and the CCA Garden are public places, operated according to Montréal Park Department standards, but maintained by the CCA.[16]

For me it was also essential that the CCA landscape express a fundamental relationship between nature and the city. Peter Rose laid out the form of the landscape, the relationship of treed and open spaces. I asked Diana Gerrard and Gunta Mackars to develop a landscape based on the ecology of the area. A study was made to identify the three historical periods of plant association: the native plants, the plants introduced by European settlers, and the cultivars (species genetically altered to produce particular characteristics, for example [fig. 19]).

The microclimate of the site was mapped to determine the effects of wind, sun, and shade, and the environmental stresses of a contemporary northern city. These include the sensitivities of plants to salt used for melting snow and ice, and to air pollutants. Trees and plants of the three historical periods of plant association were

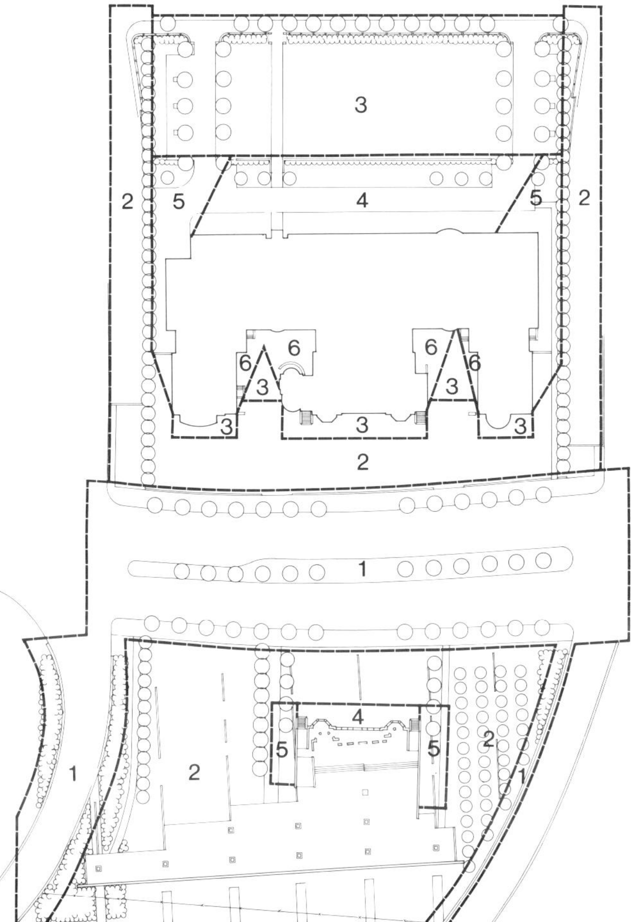

Zone	Environmental Stresses	Vegetation Types
1	exposed to wind and salt full sun very dry	cultivar
2	exposed to wind and salt full sun dry	introduced, cultivar
3	partially protected from wind full sun dry	native
4	partially protected from wind partial shade moist	native, introduced
5	exposed to wind partial shade moist	introduced, cultivar
6	protected from wind partial shade moist	native

fig. 19 The environmental stresses of the CCA landscape. Drawing: Claude Cormier, Judy Gorton, 1988. Adapted from Gerrard and Mackars Landscape Architects, "Preliminary Landscape Report: CCA," 27.

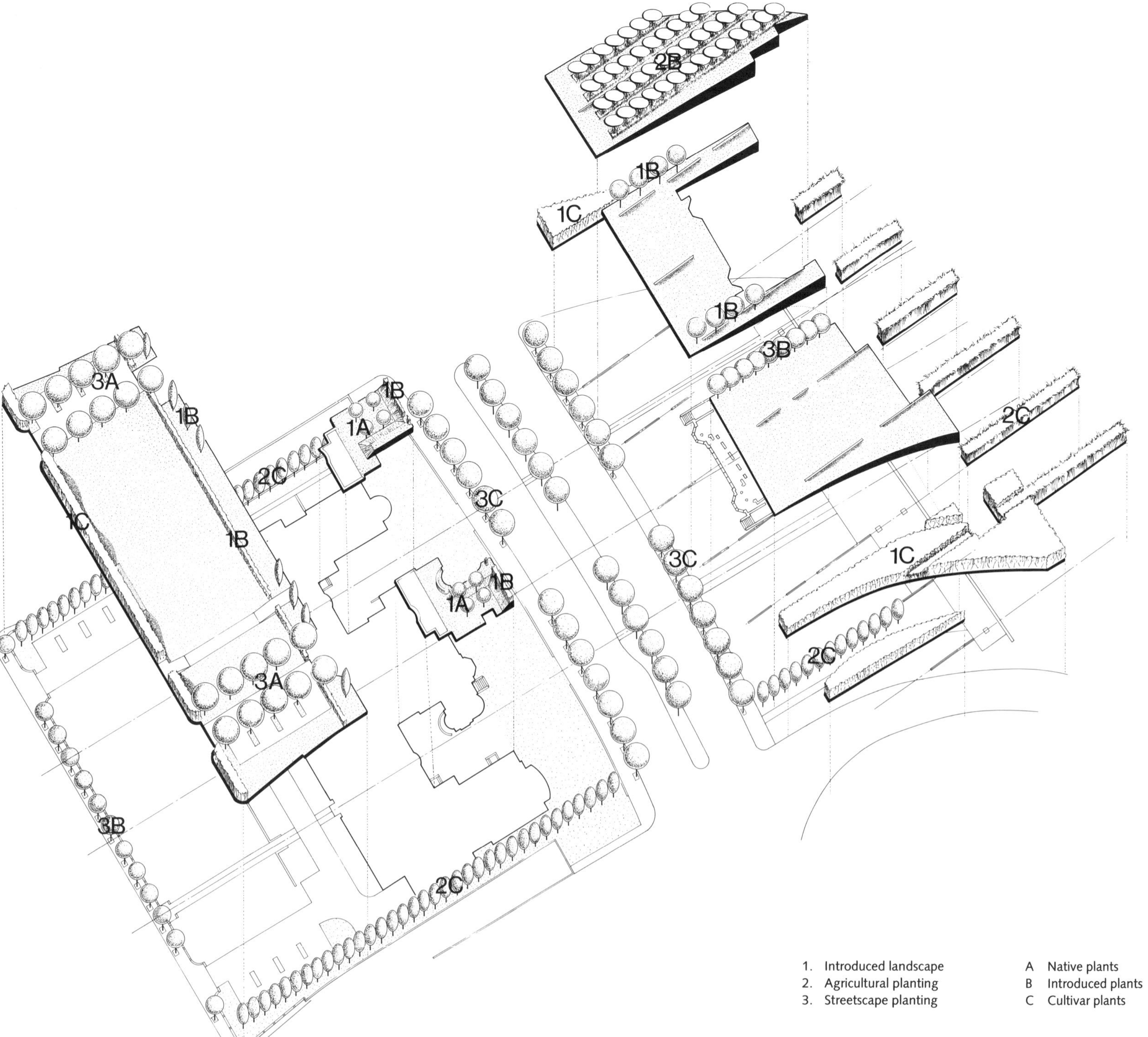

fig. 20 The planting related to the environmental stresses of the CCA Garden by Melvin Charney and Baile Park by Peter Rose. Drawing: Robert Allen, Judy Gorton, 1988. Adapted from Gerrard and Mackars Landscape Architects, "Preliminary Landscape Report: CCA," 26.

located within the appropriate microclimate and according to the design. The result was in three ecological types – forest edge, meadow, and orchard – each reflecting the particular and specific structure of individual plants (fig. 20).[17]

In a preliminary report, Gerrard and Mackars described the site as "re-presenting its own botanical history in a shortened and idealized manner," an approach they termed "regionalist," and a broadening of the realm of landcape architecture "into discourse with other areas of design theory involved in the same [architectural] investigations."[18]

The commission for the garden sculpture was awarded through a competition for the integration of art and architecture, held under a programme established by the ministère des Affaires culturelles of Quebec.[19] The CCA had proposed that the locus of the competition be the garden because of its visibility and public accessibility. The sculptors chosen to compete were qualified by their interest in site-specific art. The competition offered the opportunity to involve the whole site, a possibility that Melvin Charney's design expressed.

Charney's CCA Garden metaphorically re-represents the CCA. It resumes the design issues engaged by the building and in so doing, deeply embeds the ideas they represent. Like the building, the garden is both non-sited and sited in design. The taxis or disposition of formal elements, whole–part relationships, and issues of light and procession apply to gardens as well as to buildings. In the fine tradition of European eighteenth-century narrative gardens, the CCA Garden is composed of sections: the orchard, the field, the Shaughnessy House as a "folly," and a series of allegorical columns. In these columns, industrial chimneys below the escarpment become column and obelisk in homage to Alberti; the twin towers of a church below are represented by the archaic symbol of bulls' horns; the grain elevator is transformed into a temple; and the traditional Montréal house becomes Le Corbusier's Domino House: a history of architecture and of meaning.

The garden is profoundly located in the history of site and city. Orchard, fields, and esplanade overlook the vast stretch of river and city; it is the picturesque Sulpician Domain of Isaac Weld. The ancient dialectic of the *paradis terrestre* and the industrial city "below the hill" give the allegorical columns another level of

meaning. The nearly 2.7-metre-high column bases can be seen, as Charney describes them, as workers' houses weighted down by church and factory. Historic and modern sites, Sulpician Domain and highway, are conflated in the westernmost column. Cadastral divisions are made manifest in half-emerging lines of stone markers. Finally, the arcades, Charney's arcadian reflection of the Shaughnessy House, and beyond it the allegorical columns, propound their discourse on architecture and the city. Together they symbolize the CCA as a centre for conserving and interpreting the documents of architecture – emblems of the humanist tradition.

---

1 The space requirements for collections storage, and exhibitions and collections services changed as follows from 1980 to construction in 1988.

Area in square metres

	1980	1984	1988
Total area	6 850	10 529	13 935
Collections storage	1 375	3 530	3 753
Exhibitions	537	799	752
Conservation and photo services	237	260	386

2 The Shaughnessy House was classified federally as an historic site in 1973 and provincially as a *monument historique* in 1974, one hundred years after its completion. Its designation as a *monument historique* stopped the wave of destruction in Montréal (so reminiscent of the war-torn cities of Europe). Under Quebec law, this designation protects all buildings within a perimeter of 152 metres from the outer edges of the classified monument, thus maintaining an appropriate – or at least controllable – context, and securing the neighbourhood.

3 The concept has been widely applied. Mies van der Rohe explored the possibilities of universal space for a variety of building types, beginning with projects for a concert hall and a Museum for a Small City in 1942; and in the twenty years following for performance spaces, libraries, convention halls, houses, and office buildings. Toward the end of his career he built two such museum spaces: Cullinan Hall in the Museum of Fine Arts, Houston (1958); and the New National Gallery, Berlin (1963). Notable built examples by other architects are SOM's Beinecke Rare Book and Manuscript Library, Yale University (1965), and Piano and Rogers's Centre Georges Pompidou in Paris (1977). My own Saidye Bronfman Centre in Montréal (1968) was also conceived within the tradition of universal space.

4 The exhibition was also shown at the Centre Georges Pompidou, and the National Gallery of Canada, Ottawa, in 1984.

5 The research group, *Le Groupe de recherche sur les bâtiments en pierre grise de Montréal* (GRBPGM) systematically recorded some seven thousand notarial documents concerned with land and building transactions of the walled eighteenth-century city and its suburbs.

6 Archives nationales du Québec à Montréal, greffe [clerk] Henry Griffin, 2 Sept. 1813, no. 316. The contracts are listed in the *Catalogue of Building Contracts, 1800–1830* (Canadian Inventory of Historic Buildings).

7 Mathurin Jousse, *Le secret d'architecture découvrant fidèlement les traites géométriques, coupés et dérobements nécessaires dans les batiments …* (La Flèche: Griveau, 1642); Jean-Marie Pérouse de Montclos, *L'architecture à la française* (Paris: Picard, 1982).

8 Pehr Kalm, *Travels into North America, Containing its Natural History …*, 2nd ed., trans. John Reinhold Forster (London, 1772).

9 Antoine Desgodets, *Les lois des bâtiments …* n.p., 1777, xxii. "*Fruit*," a term used by workmen but properly "*frit*" according to Desgodets, was an almost imperceptible batten given to the front wall of a building to counteract the loads. In Montréal building contracts this "*fruit*" at times took the form of a small step back.

10 The term "*paradis terrestre*" was used by soeur Sainte-Ursule, *Mémoires*, 1:30, archives de la Congrégation de Notre-Dame de Montréal, cited by Robert Lahaise, *Les édifices conventuels du vieux Montréal* (Montréal: Hurtubise, 1980), 292.

11 In the decade after their founding in 1641 the séminaire de Saint-Sulpice acquired an elegant manor house at Issy-les-Moulineaux, Hauts-de-Seine, France, in 1655, which had been the *maison de plaisance* of Marguerite of Valois (1553–1615) Queen of France and Navarre. Its gardens, orchards, and woods, were celebrated in a long poem, "Le petit Olympe d'Issy" by Michel Bouterous (qtd. in Pierre Boisard, *Issy, le séminaire et la compagnie de Saint-Sulpice* [Paris: Esquisse Historique, 1942], 9–15). In a letter to Vachon de Belmont, Louis Tronson, third superior of Saint-Sulpice in France, expressed his hopes that the mission property, too, would become a *maison de plaisance*: "car une basse-cour si bien garnie, un colombier avec tant de pigeons, un vivier couvert de canards, d'oies et d'outardes, un beau verger rempli de tant de beaux arbres, et une si belle fontaine pour achever l'embellissement du lieu ne contribueront pas peu à lui donner tous les agréments qu'on peut souhaiter dans un village des Sauvages" (qtd. in J.-Bruno Harel, *Montréal: artisans, histoire, patrimoine* [Montréal, 1979], 24). The château de Belmont – or "Priests' Farm" as it came to be known – eventually did serve, like Issy, as a retreat for the Sulpician directors and seminarians.

12 Isaac Weld, *Travels Through the States of North America, and the Provinces of Upper and Lower Canada during the Years 1795, 1796 and 1797*, 4th ed. (London: 1800), 225–26.

13 The term "city below the hill" was established in Herbert Ames Brown's *The City Below the Hill*, (Montréal, 1897). Brown, a lawyer, documented the foul housing and living conditions of the workers in this area in order to pressure for housing reform in the city.

14 Robert Smithson describes the virtues of such a site for the landscape artist: "The site of Central Park was the result of urban blight – trees were cut down by the early settlers without any thought of the future. Such a site could be reclaimed by direct earth-moving without fear of upsetting the ecology. My own experience is that the best sites for earth art are sites that have been disrupted by industry, reckless urbanization, or nature's own devastation" ("Frederic Law Olmsted and the Dialectical Landscape," *The Writings of Robert Smithson, Essays with Illustrations*, ed. Nancy Holt [New York, 1979], 124).

15 Baile Park replaces Strathcona Park. The land of the former Strathcona Park and all other lots in the block which were not part of the Shaughnessy House property were donated to the CCA by the City in a resolution of the City Council of 20 June 1984, on the understanding that the CCA would create and maintain a green space. Rue Baile is named for Joseph-Alexandre Baile (Bayle [1802–88]), educator and superior of the Séminaire de Saint-Sulpice in Montréal.

16 The emphyteutic lease of seventy-five years (*bail emphytéotique*) between the City of Montréal and the CCA was adopted by a resolution of the City Council on 16 October 1986. The lease was signed 3 November 1986. The lease implants all rights of land ownership for the stipulated period; the grant requires that improvements be made to the land for a stipulated sum. In the case of the CCA, the garden is the improvement.

17 Ecologically, a maple-beech forest community is natural to the climatic zone of Montréal and an elm-ash-oak climax forest is specific to the Dorchester Plateau on which the CCA is located. Introduced Norway maples (*Acer platanoides*) are used by the city as street trees because they are resistant to salt, drought and heat, soil compaction and pollutants; they will border the east–west boulevard René-Lévesque, continuing the city's scheme of planting there. The north–south direction will be differentiated by rows of salt resistant cultivars, green ash (*Fraxinus pensylvanica*), edging the highway ramps. The botanical community will be able to study the performance of the native sugar maple (*Acer saccharinum*) in the city and the effectiveness of controlling the acidity content of the soil in combatting the effects of acid rain. Similarly the performance of the introduced American elm (*Ulmus Americana*), now reappearing spontaneously and disease-free in the forest, will be monitored.

18 Gerrard and Mackars, "Preliminary Landscape Report: CCA," 3 February 1988, 10.

19 The winning entry, announced on 21 September 1987, was chosen by a six-member jury composed of Phyllis Lambert and Timothy Porteous of the CCA; Peter Rose, architect, of the CCA; Jean-Claude Leblond, editor of *Vie des arts*; Louise Déry, director of the Rimouski Museum; and Ghislain Papillon, representative, département des services aux artistes, ministère des Affaires culturelles.

Interview with Peter Rose
29 June 1987

CHANTAL PONTBRIAND
AND GEORGE BAIRD

CHANTAL PONTBRIAND: It would be interesting to talk about the CCA in relation to the recent phenomenon of architecture centres and museums.

PETER ROSE: I feel that it's a coincidence that architecture museums are now quite topical. I've found the CCA to be unique – really the result of a certain set of circumstances primarily having to do with Phyllis Lambert's role: Phyllis being an architect and from Montréal, Phyllis having the will and the means, Phyllis directing a complex operation and infusing the institution with her temperament and ideals. From her perspective, if Montréal needs anything, it needs architectural help.

CP: So it might be a good idea to start with the Shaughnessy House and Phyllis's decision to preserve it and expand around it. It would have been possible to do a museum from scratch.

PR: Hypothetically it would have been possible to start from scratch but in practice it wasn't. Phyllis bought the house in the early 1970s in order to save it from demolition; and for a decade she kept it, in a perilous state, from falling down, burning down, or otherwise being destroyed. She could have found another site. You know that this is not the first scheme for the CCA. There had been another proposal – a warehouse renovation. But I think that because she had invested financially and emotionally in it, and has stood for the idea of working with and around Montréal's architectural heritage, the Shaughnessy House was a given.

Many times in the middle of the night we might have wished that the Shaughnessy House wasn't there, because it generated an enormously difficult problem. We almost got rid of it inadvertently once: when we were digging the foundations for the new building, the Shaughnessy House nearly fell into the hole. There are great pictures of it sitting precariously on what looks like a peninsula. We had exposed a layer of soil which had been under many feet of earth for decades, and it started to dry out and slide.

So the givens were first, that we had to keep the Shaughnessy House, and second, that the City preferred we enter the site from somewhere other than the Dorchester Boulevard [boulevard René-Lévesque] side. Phyllis and I eventually concluded that the access would be from the other side, on Baile, because the two side streets on the east and west are cut off by expressway ramps. So we ended up with a complex south façade – a series of pieces along Dorchester which do not necessarily read as a museum. Nor is it necessary that they should, in my opinion. There are many people who question not entering from Dorchester, but we think we made the right decision. The main image of the museum is from the opposite, Baile Street side. On Dorchester the image of the new building has more to do with a sense of urban form and a scale and rhythm of pieces that relate, essentially, back to the Shaughnessy House. And there are clues that tell you that this is an institution and send you around to the other side. The Dorchester side has a kind of rhetorical, even ambiguous, presence.

The Shaughnessy House had a serious impact on the design of the entire building and the site composition. The house has quirky qualities. It's formal and symmetrical and rather grand in every respect. But at its centre lies a solid wall, a mitoyen wall; and it has not one but two entrances, one at each end. At first glance it looks like a mansion. At second glance you realize it's a pair of duplexes, two semidetached houses. The building seems to present two of everything and rarely lets you know which is the important one. The new building reflects the idea of solidity or structure at the centre and of bilateral symmetry – a frequent presentation of two of everything and a secondary presentation of the one which you should pay attention to first. In the north facade, the entrance and the library window work as a pair in that way, with the entrance dominating. The fact that the middle part of the north wall is blind has partly to do with the fact that the

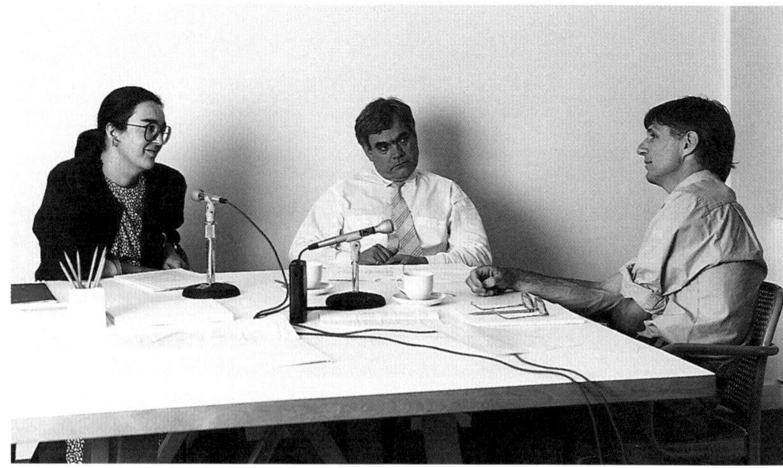

From left to right: Chantal Pontbriand, George Baird, Peter Rose. Photograph: Alain Laforest, CCA, 1987.

Shaughnessy House's central, east–west wall is solid and finally terminates in the south façade at a drainpipe embedded in those funny quoins. That quirky drainpipe had a major influence. It made it impossible for us to take anything like an entrance up the centre of the new volume; or at least it made us not want to.

CP: The way the Shaughnessy House is simultaneously separate from and integrated into the museum – more surrounded by it than integrated, maybe – suggests that the Shaughnessy House is the main exhibition piece of the museum.

PR: It depends on how you think about it. From Dorchester the view to the Shaughnessy House is open, while the flanking pieces, the auditorium and the rare book wing [Special Collections Study Room], will to some extent disappear behind rows of trees along the side streets. The planting in front of the auditorium and the rare books wing, along Dorchester, is rather dense, so the Shaughnessy House will come more and more into focus and the edges will blur. But from the other side, from Baile, where you enter, you have no sense of the Shaughnessy House at all. You can't see it. You're presented with the CCA as one fairly simple, coherent object – a wall, really – and then the Shaughnessy House unfolds episodically as you enter and go up the main stair to the little belvedere at the top where a lot of information is presented. Your position overlooking the river is made clear because you can immediately see the river and the various buildings down there such as the old Northern Electric building and a series of churches and bridges. And then in the foreground off to your left is a little piece of the Shaughnessy House … actually the most beautiful piece, the little tearoom. You see parts of the Shaughnessy House as you move into the auditorium, and you see it from the rare book room. There are little vignettes of the Shaughnessy House that are presented as one moves around within certain parts of the institution; but you never see it from the main galleries. It's presented as a whole only on Dorchester Boulevard.

CP: The role that you've given the Shaughnessy House includes functions that, in a way, respect its original programme.

PR: That was a very early intention, growing from our desire to find a way to use the house that would be sympathetic and practical. You can't put valuable works of art in the house because you can't deal with the environment in an old building; you can't make the insulation and vapour barrier good enough to control temperature and humidity. But the rooms are wonderful to sit and eat and drink in, and they have a view and the south light. It seemed like an easy fit to incorporate social rooms for reception and dining.

CP: How representative do you feel this house is of the area in which it was built?

PR: As one experiences the *quartier* now, the Shaugnessy House relates to it on several levels. For a North American city, it's a relatively homogeneous *quartier* made up of classically based greystone buildings. The Shaughnessy House has a fairly grand scale, representative of the type of building that was on the street (although other houses were grander). And it relates as well to the religious institutions on both sides of the street.

CP: Do you think the Shaughnessy House will reacquire a function in the city that is not necessarily its original function but that recalls it, is reminiscent of it? How will the building relate to the public?

PR: Even though it's almost the first thing one sees coming into Montréal from the airport, many people don't remember where it is or what it is. I think that when it is rejuvenated and surrounded by parks and flanked by two new wings, it will acquire enough

power to work with people's memory and be something that has a certain significance. We have separated the perception of the exterior from the experience of the interior because we take you away from it, around the other side, and then bring you back in. But the rooms are among the few beautifully restored nineteenth-century rooms in the city that are accessible to the public. These kinds of restorations often take place inside clubs with limited access. There are museums that have been restored – old houses that are used as museums like the Château Dufresne [Montréal] and the Cooper-Hewitt [New York]. But in the Shaughnessy House you can sit and spend time in these rooms in a more natural way – eat lunch or have tea, listen to music. I hope that the house will acquire a special meaning in Montréal – that it will penetrate the public's sense of what's theirs.

GEORGE BAIRD: I've been thinking about the CCA as a museum among museums, as we understand their evolution. I would describe it as a conservative institution by comparison with others which have recently been completed or are under construction. And that, I presume, has something to do with the nature of the collections. When I say *conservative* I mean the term in its conservationist sense, which is of course a major concern for the CCA. The issues of environmental control and of what is an artwork are in an interesting kind of relationship to one another, a relationship which is under some question at the moment. There are in fact many works of art that one could put into a non-environmentally controlled space. But I also use the term conservative in terms of issues like the sheer scale of objects which might be exhibited or stored at the CCA, and the kind of attitude to their display which is implicit in the form of the building. It would be interesting to hear you talk about those kinds of issues in relation to the design of the centre.

PR: Let's start with the environmental issue. The CCA *is* a conservative place in conservational terms. I think that most people agree that architectural collections are the most delicate, the most light-, temperature- , and humidity-sensitive of all types of museum collections. The housing of works on paper presents the worst set of standards for an architect. The light levels allowed are around five foot-candles; for things like watercolours it seems like semidarkness. And one must maintain humidity of forty-five percent, which is very damp, at a degree of constancy which puts tremendous pressure on a building, because crowds going in and out have a tremendous influence on temperature and humidity. The sun hits the walls and roofs at different times … So the CCA has, first of all, a set of requirements that are tougher than those of most new museums, and, to exacerbate the situation, the Montréal climate is extreme. There is a huge difference between Montréal's climate and New York's or Stuttgart's. We have a temperature range of more than one hundred degrees Fahrenheit. There is a story that struck a chord of fear at the CCA – whether a nightmare or a true story, I can't remember – of a Mies van der Rohe drawing that just tore one night while on exhibit in Montréal.

So the nature of the climate and the nature of the collections require, for example, that the structure of the building be separate from the exterior cladding. This building is built like the Texas meatpacking coolers that had those wonderful Maison Domino mushroom capital columns and flat slabs and then a four-foot-thick wall of brick with three feet of air sandwiched around the perimeter. One of the reasons that the CCA building volume is simple is so that we could rigorously and rationally fulfill all of the difficult environmental requirements that we were being asked to address.

GB: You have taken one step that might be thought rather daring with respect to works on paper, and that is that you have allowed for some indirect light from above.

PR: Light is very important in the conception of the building, both in terms of its exterior and in the way one experiences the interiors and views the works. One intention from the beginning was to have no galleries without daylight. In my travel and research, looking at and thinking about museums, I saw two attitudes to lighting for works on paper – both of which seemed less than successful. One was to use daylight to actually light the works of art. But because you have to control the light so rigorously with louvers that open and close in immediate response to conditions in the sky, there is mechanical noise. That didn't seem like a successful solution. Nor did the other one, which is to have no daylight at all.

When I was in Italy, looking at churches, it occurred to me that architects like Borromini had inadvertently dealt with the problem with some degree of success. You can go into any of the small Borromini churches on cramped sites and see what I'm talking about. The Quattro Fontane is a good example; it's almost dark in there – three, four, five foot-candles is the norm on a good day. It's a very vertical space, and the light often comes in through very deep windows set in great thick walls, or bounces around a few times before you see it, or is just so far up and so small that the brightness doesn't bother you. But you can always get a sense of what is going on. You know whether it is a sunny day or a grey day, whether it is afternoon or morning, from the tiniest of clues.

So we embarked on a study to see if there was a way of bringing light in: not to illuminate the works, because you can't control it, but to add a certain quality related to the natural phenomenon of daylight in the galleries. The method and the devices that we use have to do with two or three perceptions – based on the principle that one perceives in relation to the eye's adjustment to a range of foot-candle intensities in a space. We may have louvers that will adjust once a day for afternoon and morning light conditions and a couple of times a season. But when the sun comes out or goes behind a cloud nothing is opened or damped down. The levels of artificial light in the galleries all change by the same percentage; but the relationships also change. You really feel the sun; you get a strong sense of connection to the outside, but your ability to look at the works is not hindered. It's like what happens when you take two colours and modify them by the same percentage with grey. You get new relationships just by modifying each colour by the same amount. It's much more dynamic than you would expect.

Another consideration was the quality of light in Montréal, particularly in the winter, when a tiny bit of relief on a vertical surface can cast a very powerful shadow. In Montréal there are many buildings with façades, some of Ernest Cormier's buildings, for example, that have tiny amounts of change in plane – quarter-inch, half-inch, one-inch – that become very powerful. The north façade of the CCA is set up for those kinds of shadows. The whole exterior of the building is thinking a lot about the light that comes quite low and from the side.

GB: So natural light is one of the principal dimensions of the viewer's experience as you conceived it here. What are some of

Peter Rose.
Photograph: Alain Laforest, CCA, 1987.

the other dimensions? What do *you* think an architectural collection actually is? What kind of assumptions did you make about the largest possible thing that could be exhibited?

CP: That's a very important issue in the design of art museums – the problems that architects have in dealing with what will be exhibited. What about large-scale installation works which might be exhibited in a museum of architecture?

PR: That's a really deadly argument that architects always get into in making museums …

GB: What I am suggesting is that there are some assumptions about characteristic architectural artifacts which would imply that the spaces are somewhat miniaturized.

PR: Most architectural things – works, drawings, models, photographs – are relatively small. The galleries are generally eleven feet to the spring point of a cove, and then they're as high as twenty feet in the middle. They can take large objects. But we assumed that most of the objects will be small. One consideration was to keep the scale of the place down. And in trying to control light, smaller spaces are easier than bigger spaces. We've looked through the collections, gone through some of the exhibitions that are coming up for the next six years, and tried to find the biggest objects to see if the pieces will fit. And we've designed some walls to be knocked out and moved around.

If anything, the worry was that things would be *too* large. You can't leave an exhibition of works on paper up for longer than three months, which is very short. This means you are constantly taking down and putting up exhibitions. You can leave paintings up much longer, and museums tend to do that. So if the museum's too big you have to make too many exhibitions.

GB: Are there other issues bearing on the display of an architectural collection that you think influenced what you did?

PR: We considered how we express the way we've *made* the building so that it will be evident to someone looking at the building carefully. Everything isn't rational but there's a logic running through the way that the whole place is made, and by looking at it carefully enough that logic can be divined and understood. There's a logic in the way the building is planned and a hierarchy that has to do with the movement of people, with the relatively public nature of certain things, and with the relatively private nature of other things. As you move through you aren't jerked back or surprised by security measures that let you know that you've gone into a private part of the building. Generally, you experience the most public spaces first, and as you move in you get to things which will reveal themselves to be more and more private. The really private things you'll have to ask to see and will have to have someone show you how to find.

GB: Which leads me to another question, because there's another way in which I read the CCA as a conservative institution. In a recent article Douglas Crimp wrote about the phenomenon of the museum as a temple or as a treasury. I suppose the Pompidou Centre in a way represents an idea of twenty years ago of a museum as something with a commitment to radical accessibility – with a different attitude to the relationship of the public to art. And it seems to me that your description of the progressive degrees of entry into this institution, some parts of which you never see at all, places the institution within a museum tradition where the temple / treasury analogy is quite explicit and the question of accessibility relatively secondary.

One possible critique of the CCA building is that it's not accessible enough, and another one is that it has the effect of institutionalizing consciousness. What kind of position have you taken on these questions of the architectural language and the symbolic imagery of the building as they relate to its public presence?

PR: The CCA is not *radically* accessible. At the entry you've got to go through three doors just to get in. That's not very radical accessibility … it's not like the experience of the open escalator at the Pompidou Centre, where you're looking at Paris and then you can pop in and see a Renoir. I don't know how you make large numbers of fragile and valuable objects radically accessible. I understand how you can make radically accessible certain pieces of contemporary art that are made of welded steel. I think the idea of accessibility to the CCA is a tough one, given the nature of the collections. You get into all these issues of "but you have to behave," and if you have access as a scholar you still have to behave.

There's no barrier to the galleries; the bookstore and the auditorium are right there, and if people go a little further they can have tea and then go into the library. You can take them on quite a long and interesting journey, one which will unfold for them completely in the public domain. There's as much as ten thousand square feet for exhibitions if you count some of the secondary space. When you add the restaurant, the library, the auditorium, and the bookstore, close to thirty thousand square feet is accessible to the public. My feeling is that we can perhaps have the best of both worlds by accepting that people will know there is more to the CCA than what they see on the main floor.

GB: In a way, you're using the technical imperatives of conservation as a rationale for symbolism. Let me be deliberately provocative: a large number of writers and critics on art seem to be engaged in an effort to get art out of the museum or to attack the museum phenomenon for the ways in which it predetermines the way the public receives the work. And while all that is going on in the art world you are, in a way, putting architecture – which has not hitherto had this kind of aura – into a museum in such a way that it begins to partake of the aura of art in a very traditional sense. In a way one could see the CCA as taking architectural drawings into the museum while these artists are all taking art out into the street, or at least seeking to challenge the boundary. I'd like to know whether you think one would deal with that question differently because the CCA is about architecture rather than about art in a general sense.

PR: In the context of museums which are interested in expanding their boundaries and their involvement with the public and making things accessible, I think an architecture museum is very different. Maybe we are at the very beginning of a history of this particular type of museum. Maybe architecture museums begin by assembling material for study, and the act of assembly is really what makes the CCA exist. The CCA is trying to assemble sets, whole collections of architects' *oeuvres* or a set of drawings of one building or a sequence of models or whatever, many of which were pulled apart – you have one Michael Graves drawing and somebody else has five and a few other people sold a lot of ten for a big profit. The works don't lend themselves to a totally public presentation because it's hard to put a drawing on the street or a model out in the garden. The nature of the objects that the CCA has been collecting doesn't lend itself to the walls coming down and the items being placed more in the public domain. The collections here are, with few exceptions, works that were never made to be exhibited, as distinct from paintings and sculpture, which were made to be exhibited.

The real works are cities; so in a way this is like the place you go to in the New Jersey marsh where they tell you how to interpret the birds and then they take you on tours and you go look at the birds. This is an interpretive centre; the actual works are beyond the walls of the institution. The point of the CCA, which is a study centre as well as a museum, is to get you to go back out with your newfound knowledge and look at the city.

CP: The only relationship with Beaubourg that I see is the fact that the CCA library will be so important. The Centre Pompidou is not only a museum where you go to see works of art; it's also a library. On the other hand, maybe the Musée national d'art moderne, the museum part of the Centre Pompidou, is getting closer to what the CCA will be. Now that the French government has done all these renovations it has become a much more traditional museum than the free-flowing-space type of museum it was built to be ten years ago. George, the other thing you're referring to, I think, is the idea of museums without collections. Like Magasin in Grenoble, which occupies a hangar space in which it invites artists to realize projects. One could do the same thing with architects. Melvin Charney's work would be an example. At the last Documenta in Kassel ten architects were asked to come into the Orangerie, which is a castle that was turned into a museum, and do ten installations with the theme, "What would your imaginary museum be like?" It's another way of conceiving of an architecture museum, but is not necessarily the way that the CCA has been conceived. Another example, I think, would be the Strada Novissima, the imaginary street that was built in Venice a few years ago. That's another way of discussing architecture which might be different from what the CCA proposes to do.

PR: George, you mentioned another museum, the Castello di Rivoli.

GB: Yes, the Castello di Rivoli is a seventeenth-century castle near Turin, started by Juvarra but never finished. It was in ruins and then was restored in the 1960s. The result is a set of rooms of various sizes and shapes with a certain architectural precocity. The curator, Rudi Fuchs, built a collection of the kind of contemporary art he is interested in. He couldn't radically transform the spaces in the building because it is a historical monument, but he could subtly transform them, tuning them to suit a particular piece. He has an interesting mix-and-match attitude toward what piece can appropriately go in this or that space. And so you have a dialectic between the object and the space that applies to all the rooms in the castle.

PR: One could also decide that the building itself is an installation and some deconstruction could be encouraged to expose guts and structure and things which in general we don't expose. That's another legitimate and interesting idea and something that interests me. But it's not the direction that this building has taken; if it had I think it would have reflected a different position from the very beginning.

CP: Earlier you talked about the importance of the landscaping. Could you expand on that?

PR: The City of Montréal and the current condition of the city have influenced the way this building was designed, from my perspective and also from Phyllis's. Phyllis is very involved in this city and very concerned about its condition. The CCA building and its landscape comment on two things: the city's history, and its current state of decay and disintegration. In fact, I joke with Phyllis that one of the subjects of this building is native species. The stone is Quebec limestone, no longer available in Montréal; the

George Baird.
Photograph: Alain Laforest, CCA, 1987.

metal is aluminum from Alcan. The wood in the building will probably be maple and birch, and the trees are species which once grew in the area. We researched the ecology.

Of all of the things that have happened to this city, one of the saddest is the fact that the landscape is virtually gone. The trees have almost all died. The parks have been turned into green space, whatever that implies, and almost no one is thinking carefully about what urban landscape is about – either its importance or about making it. Therefore, the landscape of this project deals first with the streets, even the sidewalks. We're going to replant Baile Street with elms, which we can now use again, and we're going to replant Dorchester. The landscape, like the building, is also about the traditional organization of the city and of parcels of land that the city is made of – the cadastral lots. The city always consisted of frontage on the water, to the south, mostly, and property lines going infinitely to the north, up into the mountain and off into the sky. The building and the landscape deal with certain lines which go to infinity north and south, and things that move east and west that are contained by, that stop at, various lines – cadastral axes. So the depressed expressway ramps, which mess up the sides of the site, have been planted with a very dense row of trees, not unlike the row of trees that was on the site a few generations ago, to represent the property division before there was a division made by the street. Those lines, and a pair of lines which run through the two major north-south apertures in the building, are lines around which the organization of the landscape starts. They generate a divided centre and two flanking pieces for the CCA Garden to the south, across Dorchester, and Baile Park to the north.

Baile Park will have a simple, blank lawn at the centre, facing a blank piece of wall. This will be the public outdoor space on the north, physically and symbolically the CCA entry garden. The space is designed to create some privacy, to create a foreground, a series of edges around which one can sit, and also to obscure the flanks of the building to some degree, exposing the middle a little bit more.

On the other side, across Dorchester, we're actually lifting the ground just enough so that from grade you see not the highway, but the historic view of church steeples. Originally, the Shaughnessy House was sited to take advantage of that long view.

We've tried to come to grips with what a modern landscape is. One of the things that is clear is that we have to plant differently now because we cannot have the hordes of gardeners that people did when they were doing parks or gardens eighty or a hundred years ago. We also know a lot more now about what grows where and how and what it will do over time.

GB: And what about the seasonal sense?

PR: There's much more botanical and general technical knowledge than there used to be, so we're trying to plant with an understanding of relative rates of growth and what things will look like at certain periods and seasons. We're trying to make places that will offer shade when you want shade, shelter when you want shelter, and some protection from the wind.

We're carefully playing with colour. The major trees will be elm, sugar maple, and ash. The elm will grow very high and branch starting quite high; the maple will have branches starting much lower and will not grow as high. We're probably going to top the maples a little bit, compress them. Ash is much more ragged along the edge, branching almost down to the bottom; it will be planted with material that will have a similar leaf pattern and will almost make a wall.

We're trying to develop drawing techniques to study landscape. In any case, the landscape is like a laboratory and will be worked on

Chantal Pontbriand.
Photograph: Alain Laforest, CCA, 1987.

over time. We intend it to have a very strong relationship with the building and with the history of the place, and to be an example for the rest of the city.

CP: This concern with developing a landscape for the context that you're working in – the Canadian climate, the city environment of the museum (a very harsh one with the autoroute near it): is it a preoccupation of yours to develop a Canadian architecture or an architecture typical of Montréal?

PR: I'm naturally an intuitive person. I operate by intuition and then try to look afterward and see what the theory was rather than developing a theory at the beginning. I've always spent a lot of time walking around a site looking at similar things and thinking, intentionally, but in a nonstructured way, thinking about what connections can be made and what oppportunities there are in the site. I always feel the need to develop a knowledge of a place – to acquire a set of instincts that will operate through the process of design. That's the intuitive side.

Over the past decade I've also been a serious student of this city, of certain buildings in it and of other places that relate to it. It's not a random study. I'm preoccupied with the idea that there is a subtle range of things that cause buildings to fit and feel like they're part of a place and have a sense of that place. It's tough to do, and it's tougher to do now in the fragmented urban landscape than it was in the past, for example, in the nineteenth century. But Montréal buildings like the Royal Bank, the Gleneagles, and the Trafalgar on the mountain; and Rockefeller Center in New York have that sense of belonging. There are others that had to meet a challenge to find ways of fitting: the Yale Art Gallery addition by Kahn, for example, which is a very modern piece next to a quite beautiful nineteenth-century art gallery. I'm fascinated by how one makes relationships and how one embeds a building in a place.

I first became fascinated by fit and place when I was thinking about building houses. I realized that many contemporary houses looked great in photographs, but in reality seemed awkward, and tentatively connected to site and landscape and view. By contrast, almost every farm building or cluster of farm buildings I ever saw seemed so firmly embedded in climate, topography, and landscape that I began to think that if farmers can do it, and if mediocre architects in the nineteenth century could do it, there was *something* that they were doing. My sense was that they were simply taking more time and smelling and listening and looking and coming back at night and coming back in the winter and just getting a feel for the place. This building – its size, its placement, the materials, the classical language of it (that's more willful, maybe), the use of those axes that are part of the way the city is organized, the lines that go through all the way from the river to the mountain – it's all part of a sense that I've acquired from looking at the Shaughnessy House site for ten years.

The CCA building deals primarily with the nineteenth- and early twentieth-century Montréal context and ignores to some extent what's happened more recently. That's just willful ignorance. One other relevant point is that the image, in plan, of the central piece with the flanking wings and something connecting it, is typical of the way all the major institutional buildings are built in Montréal – particularly the church buildings. If you look at a plan, a figure-ground, of the surrounding area of the city, you'll see a series of generic institutions, most of them religious. This building just disappears in that. The CCA relates to these large institutions through its plan and massing. But it's kept low and has a certain scale that relates also to its more local neighborhood.

GB: One reads the CCA as having a calm and sobriety which is something of a departure from the more picturesque, elaborate character of your earlier projects.

PR: It's a sobering experience to do a building that's going to last this long. It imparts a certain attitude and tone to one's work. And the fact that everything is being subjected to the hundred-year test is significant. When someone presents a detail or a piece Phyllis asks, "Will this last a hundred years?" When you start thinking in those terms, you look at your ideas from five years ago and evaluate which ones have held up and which ones haven't. It all has to do with the evolution of one's thought. When you do a commercial building, you want to it be like fashion. When it hits the streets it has to be really hot and deal with all of the issues of the day. The CCA is completely the opposite. It's very important that the building be durable, aesthetically or architecturally, as well as physically. So it has become fairly restrained. There's a lot of elaboration to make the building less sober, a little bit more abstract and more modern. I hope that it comes alive as the last things go on and in – the cornice, the metalwork, and the aluminum fence. The light on the stone wall will be extraordinary because, although it is made of simple pieces, the cornice casts very complex shadows. I think it's important that the CCA design steer clear of gestures that seem wonderful for a few years but not so wonderful over time.

Portfolio 2

Drawings by the office of
Peter Rose Architect, 1988

Site Plan of the CCA, including the CCA Garden

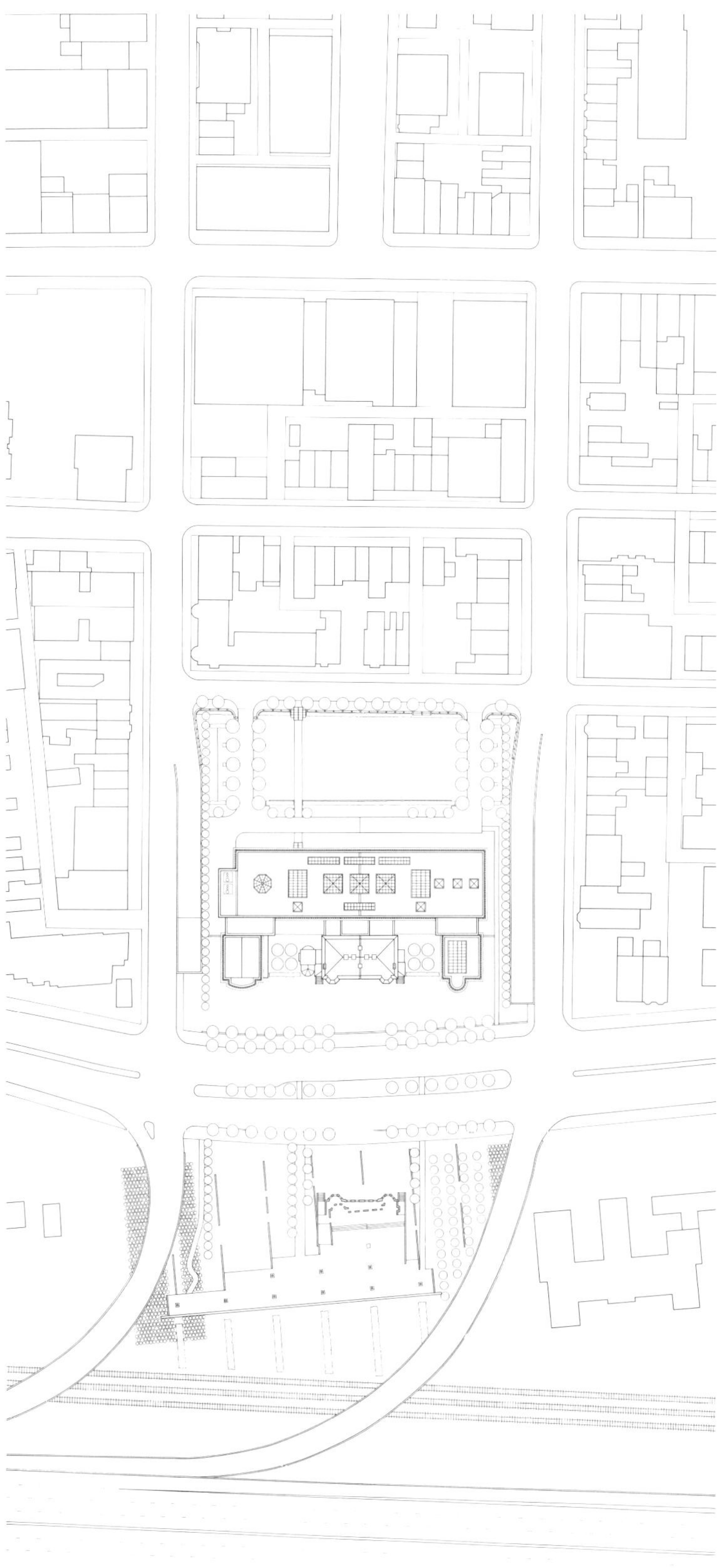

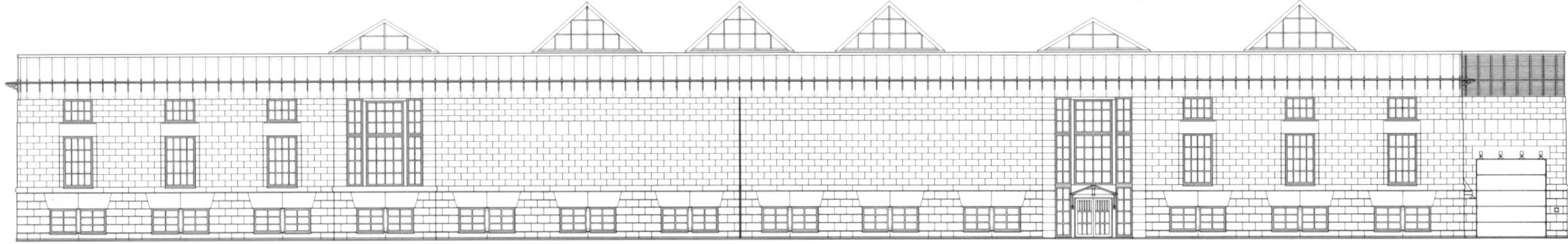

North Elevation

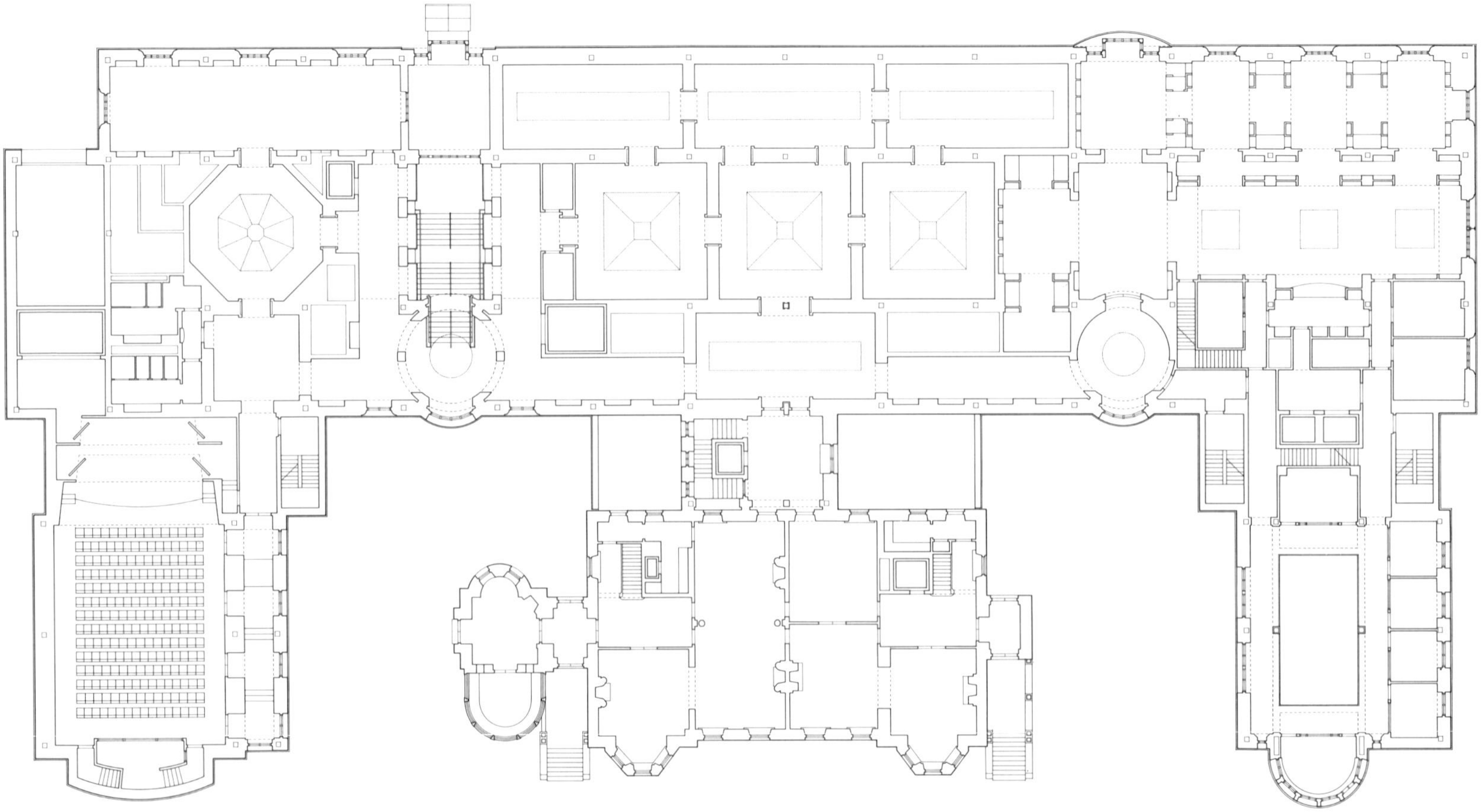

Plan of the Public Level

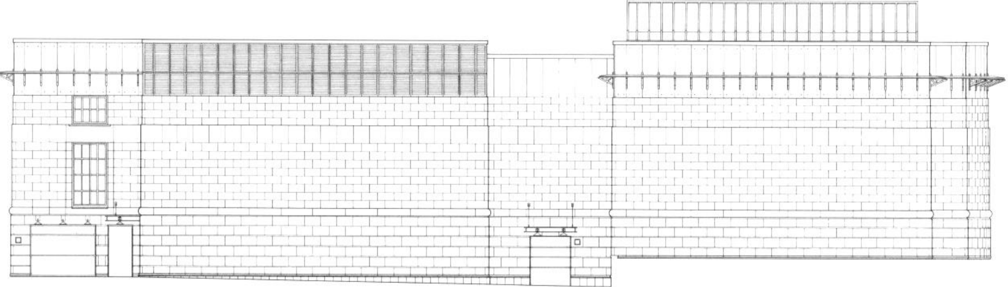

West Elevation

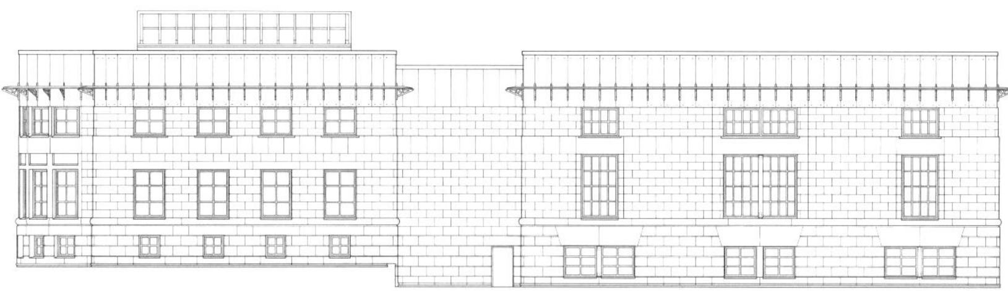

East Elevation

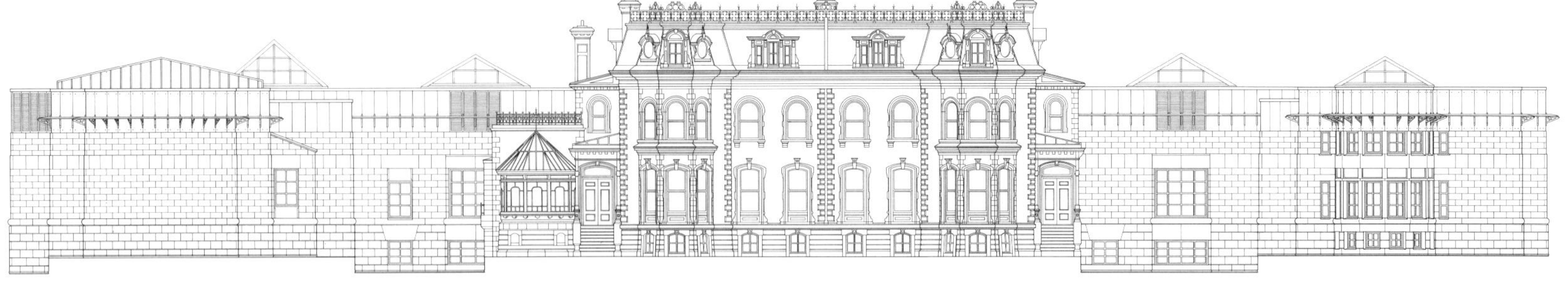

South Elevation

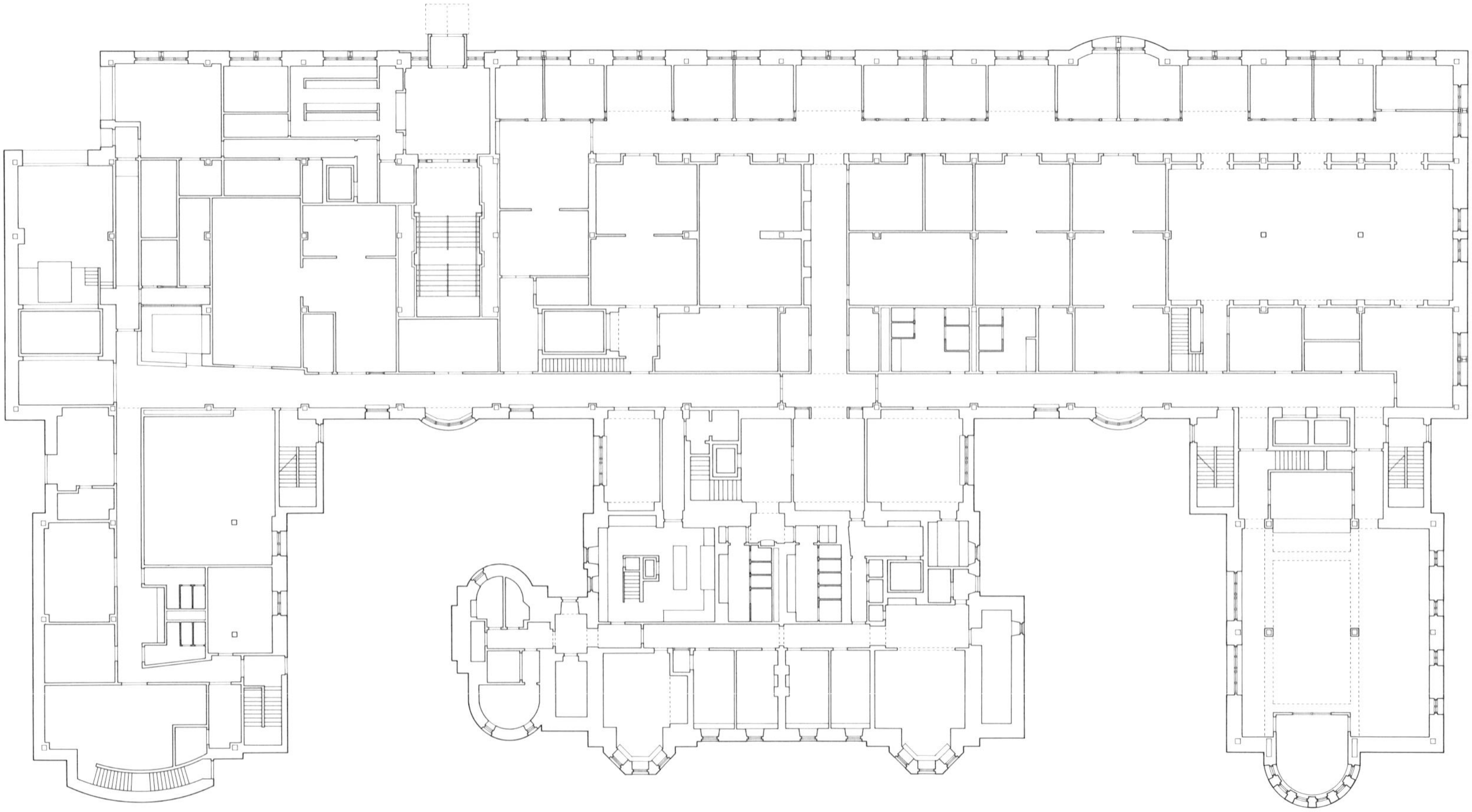

Plan of the Curatorial Level

Transverse Section

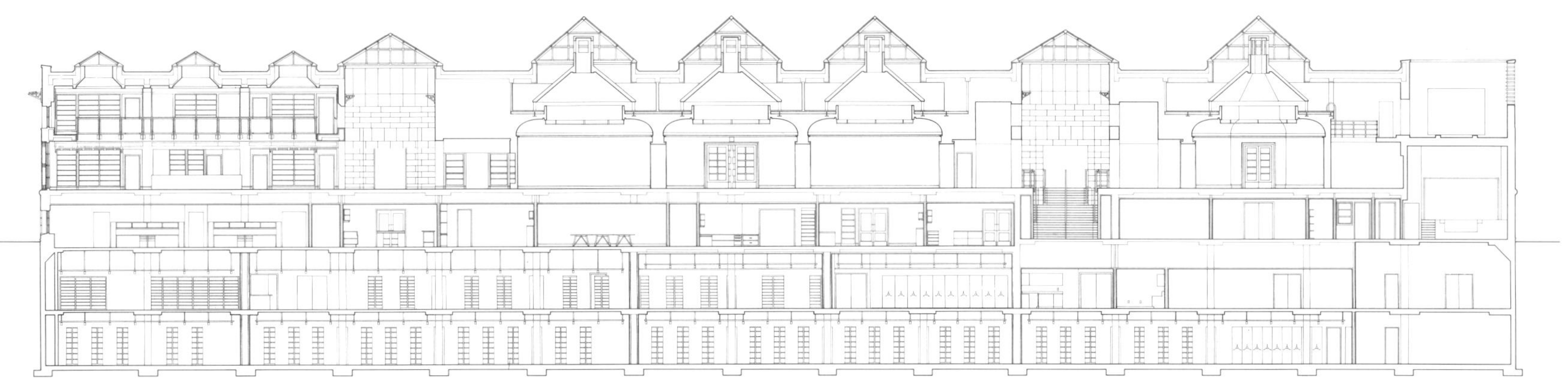

Longitudinal Section

Exterior Wall Detail

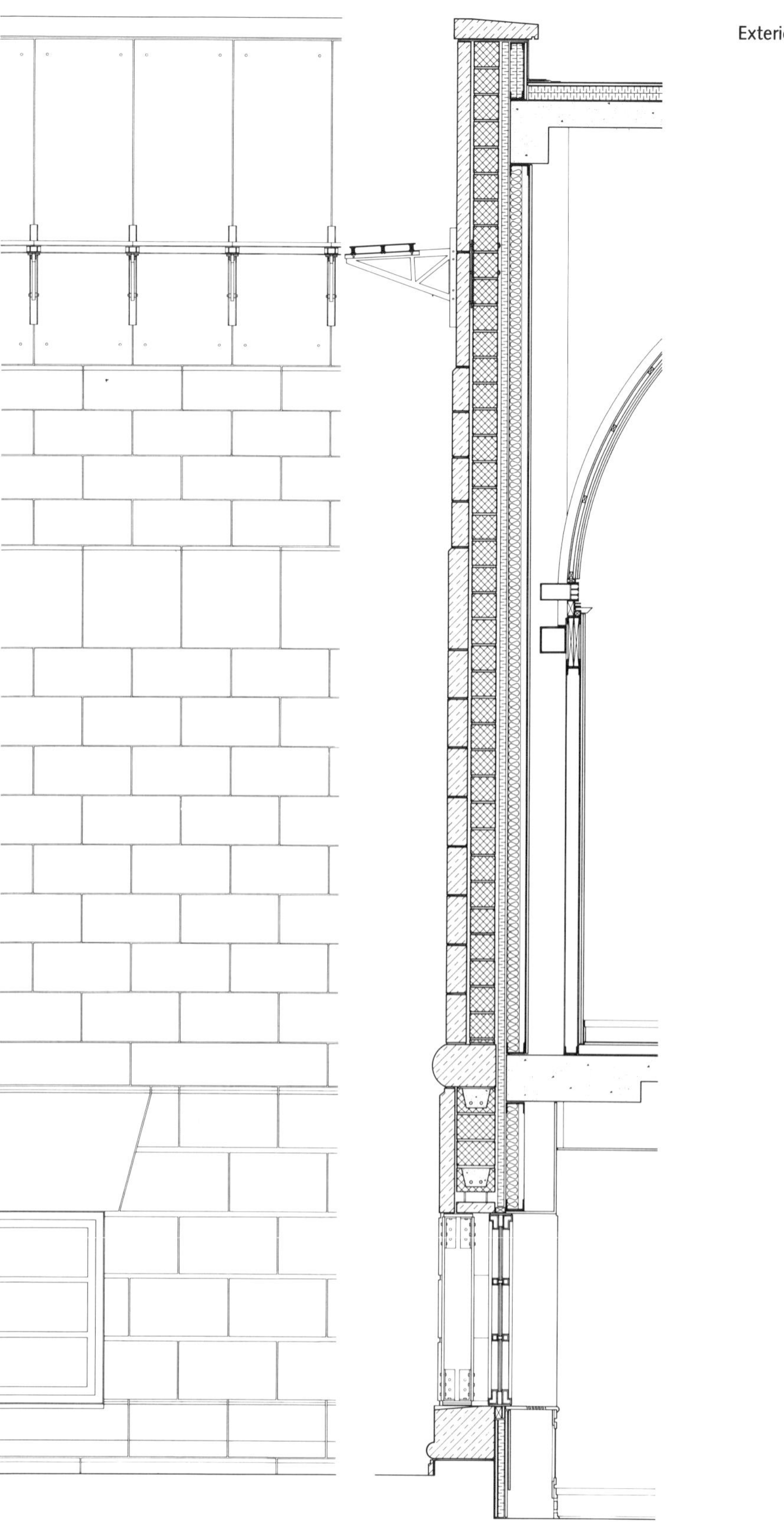

A Garden for the Canadian Centre for Architecture

MELVIN CHARNEY

How does one conceive of a public garden for an architectural museum and study centre, a garden situated on no more than a residual plot stranded between the entrance and exit ramps of an automobile expressway?

The site of the CCA Garden presented the typical contradictions of twentieth-century urban life: a derelict piece of the city left over after an expressway was pushed through its older centre. By the time the expressway – the autoroute Ville-Marie – was built in the mid-1960s, the site had already been cleared of early nineteenth-century estates and late nineteenth-century townhouses which were demolished in a post-World War II drive to modernize the infrastructure of the city, an effort that devastated the substance it was intended to renew, as if the prewar emulation of European cities had given way to an emulation of their subsequent destruction (figs. 21, 35).

The site of the garden is also typical of the location of important urban parks built since the eighteenth century, such as the parc des Buttes-Chaumont in Paris. These parks were created on residual terrain cast aside by transformations of the city. Obsolete fortifications and quarries, abandoned abattoirs, railway lines, and, later, expressways – all neglected and degraded areas caught between layers of the city – were made into ideal figures of verdure in attempts to redeem the reality of urban life.

fig. 21 *Topographical and Pictorial Map of the City of Montreal*, 1846. Cartographer: James Cane. National Archives of Canada (NMC 2053). This detail, the upper left corner of the map, shows the initial urbanization of the site of the CCA Garden, the location of Dorchester Street (now boulevard René-Lévesque), the Priest's Farm, and numerous apple orchards.

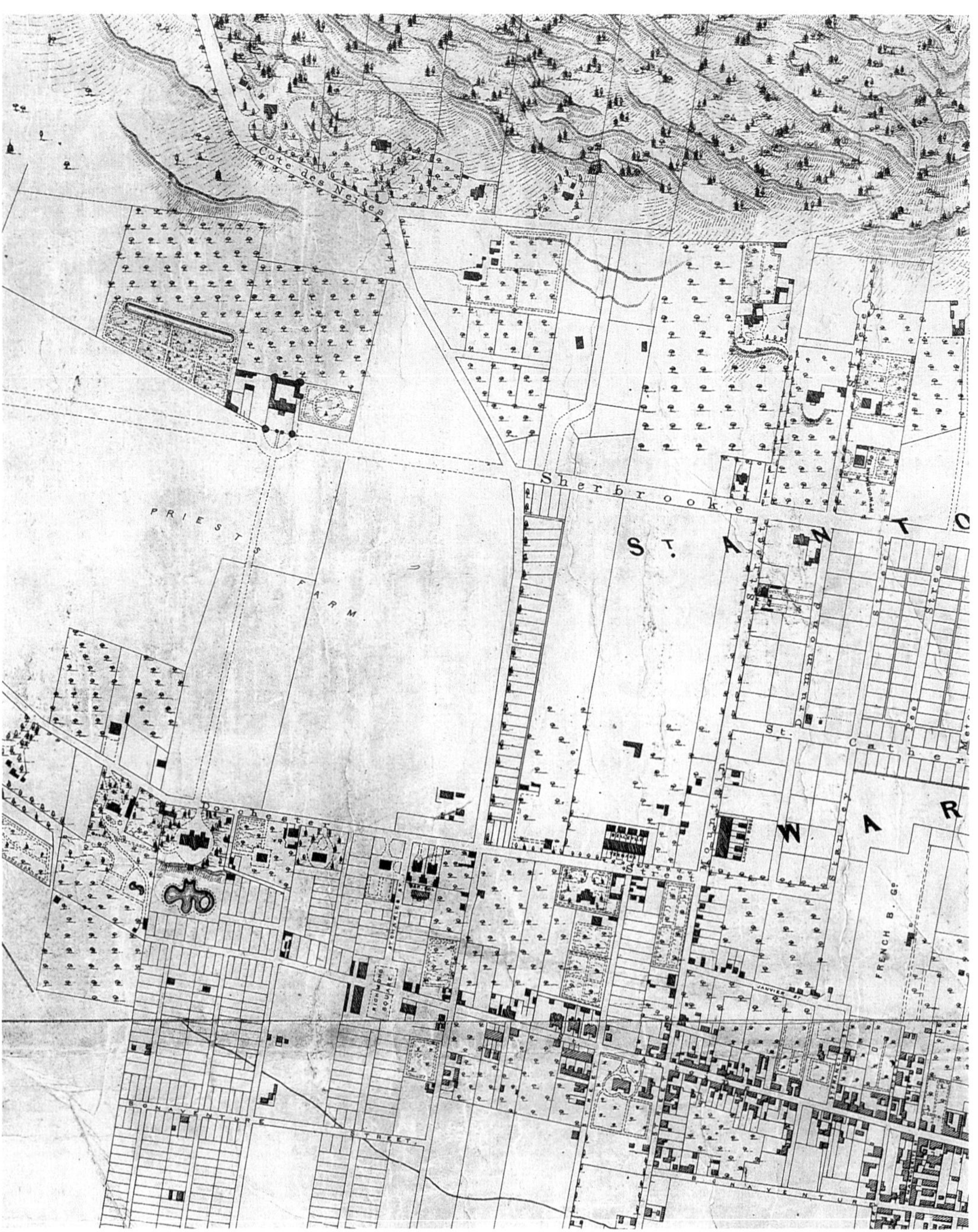

The widening of Dorchester Street (now boulevard René-Lévesque) into a boulevard in the 1950s and the subsequent construction of the autoroute Ville-Marie left few traces of the tight-knit urban structure of Montréal in the area of the site. Earth-fill and rubble were bulldozed to create a flat terrain in between two ramps of the expressway and over two traffic tunnels that pass under the site. The terrain now floats on the edge of an escarpment, a dislocated wasteland between streams of traffic set off against the horizon and the city below (figs. 22, 23).

The Garden in the City

The very idea of a garden confronted the marginal condition of the site and its relationship to the city. The site exists as an urban fact. It embodies concrete traces of human passage rooted in history and memory, layer upon layer. The layers of history have neither a past nor a future; they are simply there to be dragged up as a measure of the place, a map of its ongoing transformation.

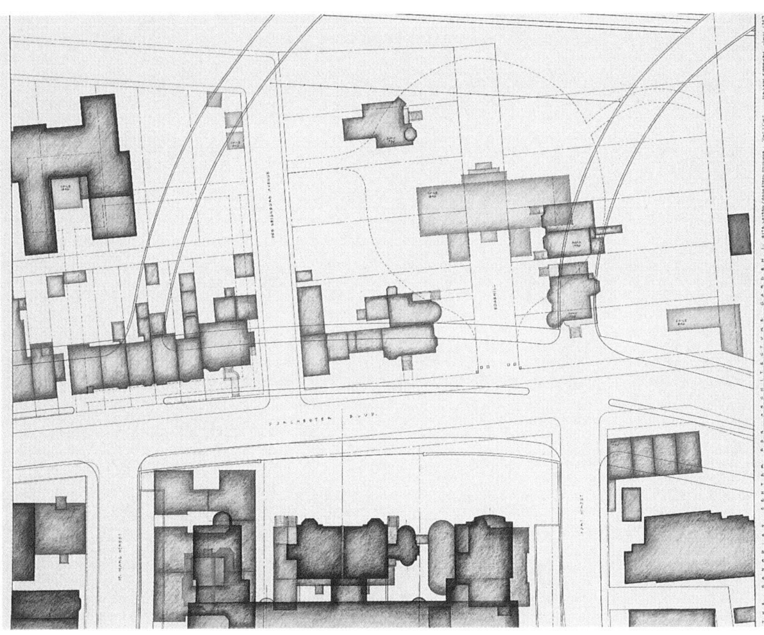

fig. 22   Melvin Charney, *The historical layers of the CCA Garden site between 1800 and 1950*, 1986. Coloured pencil and ink on vellum.

fig. 23   The future site of the CCA Garden. Photograph: Michel Boulet, CCA, 1986.

The layers of memory, however, are ever-present. They cut deep, transcend place and time, and summon forth typologies of an ideal city and models of rural idylls and Arcadian forest edge.

Even though the site was a ruin, its situation is magnificent. It is located on a major east–west thoroughfare and on a prominent escarpment that marks the edge of a plateau – both important features of the city. To the south, the escarpment overlooks the remains of nineteenth-century factories and working-class neighbourhoods, a panorama which opens out to the St. Lawrence River and to the mountains beyond. The site thereby affords a direct encounter with the horizon and the landmass of the city, and along with the presence of Mount Royal to the north, above the CCA building, it also reveals a sense of Montréal as it was originally settled, between the river and the mountain.

Given the nature of the CCA as a public institution and the formal signification of the boulevard that passes between it and the site, the creation of a public garden complementary to and directly across from the CCA establishes a north–south focus and an event in the collective order of the city. That order is suggested by the block system, by the grid alignment of streets, by the party walls between buildings, and by the remains of the organization of earlier farms in the area, all of which follow the original cadastral system of land division. The few nineteenth-century greystone buildings which survive in the vicinity of the site are the remains of an urban architecture that distinguished the area at the turn of the century. The CCA was designed around the restoration of one such surviving building, the Shaughnessy House, constructed in 1874. The site is also adjacent to a residential neighbourhood, recently revived, but with little public open space for the community.

The CCA building was in itself an urban fact to consider. Its situation on a major boulevard, with its front and main entrance on a secondary street, suggested the configuration of a typical *hôtel particulier* as it evolved in Paris in the eighteenth and nineteenth centuries. Visualize the residence of an eighteenth-century grandee, now a public institution, with its main entrance on the narrow rue du faubourg Saint-Honoré and a portico leading from the street into a walled, paved courtyard. Within the courtyard is the principal façade of the building, a front door, and, inside, a sequence of public reception rooms which open onto gardens and onto the avenue des Champs-Élysées at the back. Whereas the front of the *hôtel* is no more than a wall scaled to the enclosure of a secondary street, the back of the building appears as a series of pavilions set within the garden-like, monumental avenue, setting off a dialectic between front and back, between the figure of a house on a city street and the representation of a house in an Arcadian revision of an urban boulevard. So it is with the relationship between the CCA building and boulevard René-Lévesque. The back of the building is its urban and monumental front: the garden was conceived accordingly.

The CCA Garden thus had to respond to at least three programmatic categories: a garden that is a public and urban event related to major elements of the city; a garden related to the CCA as a study centre, archive, and museum of architecture; and a neighbourhood garden.

These gardens were established by invoking the site as an urban composition, and by invoking the formal specificity of garden architecture as a parallel text. The urban constituents of the site were then correlated to basic garden formations. In other words, the formal constituents of a garden were taken to be not so much the dialectic opposites of the constituents of a city, the persistent notion, expounded by Frederick Law Olmsted, of a city park as an innocent, rural retreat, a "lung" of verdure set in "the greatest possible contrast to the restraining" city, but as the transfiguration of the city itself.

Such a garden is not scenic but scenographic. Each constituent assumes a specific form: an esplanade was made to appear in the guise of an "esplanade," a boulevard was made to be a "boulevard." This was done with the understanding that the critical operation which unravelled the "textual" composition of the site and of gardens also exposed intelligible and paradigmatic figural formations. These type formations were then situated in a referential framework that challenged their representational capacity. This was done in two ways. Each constituent of the garden was set up as the direct counterpart of an existing element of the city that could be seen, or could be made to be "seen," from the site – for example, a "façade" is placed in the garden in relation to an existing façade on an opposite street. Each

fig. 24 *Montréal in 1761.* Cartographer: Paul Labrosse, revised in 1914 by E.Z. Massicotte. Bibliothèque nationale du Québec, section des cartes. Note the extensive formal gardens attached to religious establishments within the walls of the original settlement.

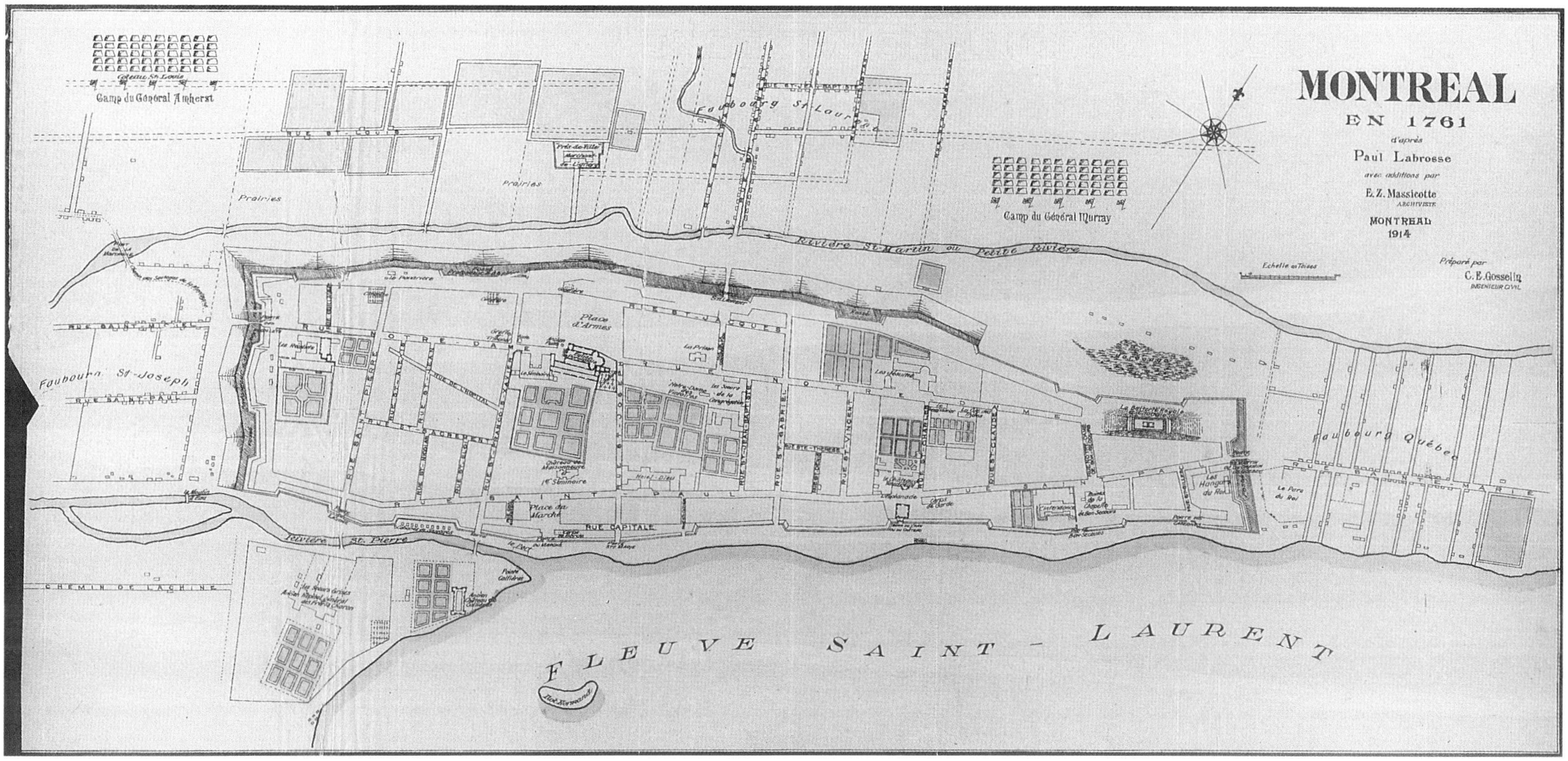

constituent was also countered in the garden by the placement of a second and analogous construct derived from the first – by the representation of the representation, so to speak – an arcade is represented by a second "arcade," for example. Each constituent of the garden is thereby tied directly to the surrounding city. And Montréal has a rich urban history which is well grounded in the tradition of city building, as well as a history of numerous formal gardens – fragments of a *paradis terrestre* – implanted in the walls of its initial settlement (fig. 24).

Central to the compositional propositions outlined above, are the three essential visions of the CCA Garden:

The "Urban Garden" is organized about two series of north–south axes drawn out of the structure of the city and superposed one on the other. The first set, parallel to the axes of the CCA building, enjoins the two sides of the boulevard. One side of the boulevard is set up as the counterpart of the other by the placement in the garden of a mirror-like reconstruction of the

Shaughnessy House in the form of an arcade. The two "houses" frame the boulevard and incorporate it into a larger composition that traverses the roadway, and joins the CCA Garden to the building in a monumental gesture. The terrain of the garden is sloped up from the boulevard, between the ramps of the expressway, so as to establish an esplanade and a belvedere on the edge of the escarpment. The rise of land enhances the escarpment, sets the landscape of the garden to the horizon, and creates a tilted-up façade whose general composition is readily perceptible to the passerby. The Garden was conceived to be a place to look at, as well as a place to look out from.

The "Museum Garden" extends the museological function of the CCA outdoors, on an urban scale and accessible to the public at all times. In the manner of a building that reveals the history of building, the garden reveals the historicity of its existence. Layers of settlement, such as older forms of land division and plant material, were made to appear. The plan of the CCA building also

fig. 25   A southwest view of the original study model of the CCA Garden. Melvin Charney, 1987.

appears; the reconstruction of the Shaughnessy House and the long *allée* of the garden esplanade correspond to the configuration of the CCA building with its long suite of exhibition galleries. Allegorical columns, situated on the esplanade, interpret the architectural signification of distinctive buildings in the surroundings, features of a city on display.

The "Neighbourhood Garden" is episodic, with defined places and objects to go to, along with bucolic delights such as a meadow and an orchard, convenient promenades, and ample seating.

The CCA Garden was thereby composed of type figures – for example, an arcade, an esplanade, a meadow, an orchard – that are set about a series of shifting organizational axes, and that cut across and sustain its diverse, programmatic requirements (figs. 25, 36).

The North–South Axes

The location of Montréal, between a river to the south and a mountain to the north, accentuates the distinction between attenuated east–west routes of access and limited north–south axes of urban activity found in the settlement of Canada. This distinction can be seen, for example, between rue Sherbrooke, which traverses the island of Montréal from east to west, and the place-des-Arts / Complexe Desjardins axis which crosses the downtown core from north to south. A similar distinction can be made between the east–west run of boulevard René-Lévesque and the autoroute Ville Marie, and the orientation of the garden in relation to the CCA building and to the city.

Two sets of north–south axes traverse the CCA Garden. The first set, already described, aligns the composition of the garden with that of the CCA building. The major axis of the building is picked up by the arcade. Minor axes are drawn out along the walkways of the garden. The main walkway prolongs the entrance axis of the building; the entrance sequence to the building – fence, park, door, hall, main stair, bay window, courtyard – extends in the garden along an *allée* of trees up to the esplanade and to a view of the horizon. However, while the tripartite composition of the CCA buildings is reflected in the garden, its symmetry is displaced, its centre shifted. The axial register between the mirror-like façades on either side of the boulevard is countered in the garden by a second register of opposites situated on either side of the axis of the main walkway: on one side, the arcade, a configuration that gives body to the interior of the garden, and on the other, the meadow, which represents the garden as an exterior, rural landscape.

Early nineteenth-century maps of Montréal show that the initial urbanization of the area of the garden proceeded from the east and the south of the site up to and along the escarpment (see fig. 21). The alignment of the orthogonal lots – the cadastral subdivisions – to the south of the present-day boulevard is parallel to the run of streets emanating from the river and the lower town. The land to the north of the boulevard, however – the area that formerly made up the Sulpician Domain where the CCA building is situated – was settled at a later date along cadastral divisions that descended from and are perpendicular to rue Sherbrooke and to the mountain. This shift in the alignment of the underlying system of land division is located on the northern boundary of the site, and is reflected in the garden in the shift between the two sets of organizational axes about which it was composed: the urban grid from the north is offset from, and superposed upon, a second grid rising from the south. One grid is made to undercut the other.

fig. 26 View north along the axis of rue du Fort to the pediment of the seminary of the Collège de Montréal, from the position of column number 11 on the esplanade of the CCA Garden. Photograph: Melvin Charney, 1987.

The second series of axial alignments is grounded in the garden by a series of "cadastral" walls and by the allegorical columns that pick up on parts of the city to the north and south of the site: to the north, the remains of the eighteenth-century Fort de la montagne and the pediment of the seminary of the Collège de Montréal on the site of the old fort (figs. 26, 27); to the south, the factories, grain elevators, churches, and tenements (fig. 28).

fig. 27 Jean Antoine Watteau, *La Perspective*, ca. 1719. Maria Antoinette Evans Fund. Courtesy, Museum of Fine Arts, Boston. Watteau's painting reveals the pediment of Montmorency through the hundred-year-old trees of Le Nôtre's original layout, similar to that of the view of the seminary of the Collège de Montréal shown in figure 26.

The Shaughnessy House as an Arcade

The introduction of objects which represent existing objects – the introduction in the conception of the garden of recursive, self-reflexive devices – also introduces a register that scales the presence of one object with regard to the existence of another. This device introduces a degree of displacement of the meaning of one object in relation to another and, hence, to itself.

The reconstruction of the Shaughnessy House in the garden suggested its reappearance not as a "picturesque" or deliberate ruin, but as a building stripped of all functional overlay other than that of being "itself" in a garden, an abode in Arcadia. The "self" in the garden assumed the form of a *fabrique*, a building type inseparable from the art of gardening, an arcade in Arcadia. The Shaughnessy House was emptied of content and its envelope was sliced off in part at an appropriate height.

fig. 28 Melvin Charney, *Panorama of the City from the CCA Garden,* 1987. Photomontage.

The similarity of the two buildings establishes a direct physical and visual link which centres the CCA building and the garden upon each other. Repetition sets up a duality, a reflection of one building in the other, a mirror image. The mirror image blurs the distinction between subject and object and registers a measure of narcissism inherent in the monumental form of the city – the necessary anthropocentrism of urbanity, of the collective "self" of people reflected in the body of the city, if such still exists.

The arcade also situates the interior of the garden, represented by a second arcade set within the first. The second arcade was also created by the reconstruction of a cut-off segment of the first. And while the first arcade is aligned with the set of axes emanating from the CCA building to the north, the second is related to the set of axes drawn up from the south. One arcade is thus enclosed by and offset from the other. The repetition of the two arcades sets up a duality reflecting the duality of the two buildings facing each other across the boulevard. A repetition is thereby set within a repetition, each attesting to the presence of the other.

The Cadastral Walls

Before 1950, rue des Seigneurs extended up the escarpment from the lower town and traversed the site. There were houses along Dorchester Street and along Edgehill, a private street that extended from Dorchester to the edge of the escarpment (see fig. 22). Today, all that remains on the site of earlier buildings and streets are traces of the cadastral subdivisions which still appear on legal surveys and can still be extrapolated from buildings in the area.

The cadastral grid has its roots in the classical system of land subdivision and in the planning of cities throughout history. It appears to be less a model than a primal structure of human settlement, a series of reproducible relationships that subsume the form of a city. One of the strengths of this system is the direct relationship between the structure of rural land and the structure of the city, seen in the plans of newly implanted Greek and Roman cities, and in the Zähringer new towns – Bern, Freiburg – created in the twelfth century. The cadastral system was also implanted in Montréal where the continuity between the city grid and rural land divisions can be readily seen in the conversion of the rural *rangs* – the long and narrow orthogonal farm lots – into orthogonal city blocks, one a direct transposition of the other (fig. 29).

The layers of the cadastral grid, once located in the strata of the site, reappear in the garden as a series of walls which emerge from the slope of the terrain, below the esplanade, as if the soil had eroded away to expose an ancient structure. These walls – cadastral walls – deform the slope of the terrain as some

fig. 29 Photograph of the 1950's showing urbanization of farm rangs in Montreal.

accidental slippage. They can be seen either as the remains of the party walls on the property lines between buildings that once existed on the site – the eighteen-inch-wide mitoyen wall prescribed by laws dating back to the fourteenth-century in France – or as fieldstone walls that separated the early farm *rangs* which also existed on the site. Rural and urban strata overlap.

The Columns

"Gardens … should not be wanting of columns and obelisks" (Leon Battista Alberti in *De Re Aedificatoria*).

The placement of columns in the CCA Garden was derived, as were other devices, from a reading of historical types. In the same way as the cadastral walls "reveal" an ancient structure of land division, so the placement of herms, statues that served to mark farms and boundaries in Greek and Roman times, is recovered by the position of allegorical columns on the esplanade and in relation to the cadastral grid of the garden. These columns also reveal the situation of allegorical, columnar figures which lined garden walks, *allées*, avenues, and esplanades, in later centuries (figs. 30, 31).

An allegory is a narrative, a commentary of one text read through another, an extended metaphor. The narrative presented by the

fig. 30 The Canephori in the sixteenth-century *giardino segreto* of the Casino, Palazzo Farnese, Caprarola. Reproduced from Christopher Thacker, *The History of Gardens,* 1979.

fig. 31 The Emperor's Walk at Grimston, Yorkshire, landscaped by William Andrews Nesfield, nineteenth century. Reprinted from *Country Life,* 12 Oct. 1901. By kind permission of *Country Life.*

columns is intended to capture and objectify an architectural discourse derived from distinctive buildings, as befits a museum of architecture. As elsewhere in the garden, the columns were made to establish self-reflexive dualities. A first line of columns was set up as the direct counterpoint to and reflection of actual parts of the city, while a second line was set up as a counterpoint to and reflection of the first series of columns, echoing the first as the first echoes the architecture of the city.

The buildings which can be readily identified from the esplanade and which constitute a slice of significant architecture can be

discerned in what remains of the late nineteenth- and early twentieth-century industrial *quartiers* of the lower town, below the escarpment. The essential elements of an industrial city are evident, even though most of the factories have been abandoned and large parts of these neighbourhoods were demolished during the wave of urban "renewal" that swept across Montréal in the 1960s and 1970s. The area directly south of the site, known as la petite Bourgogne, was particularly affected. Nevertheless, the surviving buildings reveal the transposition of a proto-classic vernacular brought over to North America by settlers into an indigenous, proto-modern typology that reemerged later in the heroic period of the Modern movement in Europe. It still reverberates in our grasp of built form.

The narrative begins at the column bases, which pick up on the tenement blocks typical of the industrial *quartiers* – the houses of people whose lives were crushed by the factory and the church. Commentary on the form of the house as a type and as an archetype is woven through the sequence of columns, a subtext to the overall narrative. These "houses" are built of wood and encased in copper in the manner of local religious statuary, and inserted into columns of concrete and steel.

The narrative sequence of the columns is arranged in rows from east to west, starting with the column closest to the edge of the esplanade (fig. 37):

ROW A

Column one takes the numerous chimney stacks which rise above the factories and houses of the lower city as its subject. The prominent chimney of the Northern Electric Building in Pointe Saint-Charles is reworked into a tall shaft that speaks of obelisks, a Ledoux cannon foundry, a cenotaph, and the smokestacks of the industrial era.

ROW B

Column three interprets the form of houses found in the *quartiers* below the esplanade. This column speaks of the urbanization of the *maison québécoise*, a type of house imported from western France by the first settlers, and of its rationalization into an equally traditional urban type, the tenement, related to Roman domestic architecture. This indigenous transformation is contrasted to the rationalisation by Le Corbusier of houses in northwestern France similar to the *maison québécoise*, which gave rise to his Maison Domino.

Column four is about the legacy of modernism, a dancing "Domino" (fig. 32). Le Corbusier's Maison Domino was drawn out of column three. The tenement was freed of enclosing walls so that De Stijl-like planes now slide in and out of its floors in a seemingly liberating gesture.

ROW C

Column six picks up on the numerous grain elevators in the lower city. It also recalls illustrations which appeared in tracts of the Modern movement. Specifically, the column represents the elevator of a flour mill located on the rue Notre-Dame, directly south of the garden.

Column seven shows the grain elevators again, this time as a temple of rational architecture. This narrative reflects upon two complementary pages of Le Corbusier's *Vers une architecture*, one illustrating grain silos in Canada, the other the Parthenon in Athens.

ROW D

Column eight picks up on the twin-spired Sainte-Cunégonde church in the *quartier* immediately below the site (fig. 33). The

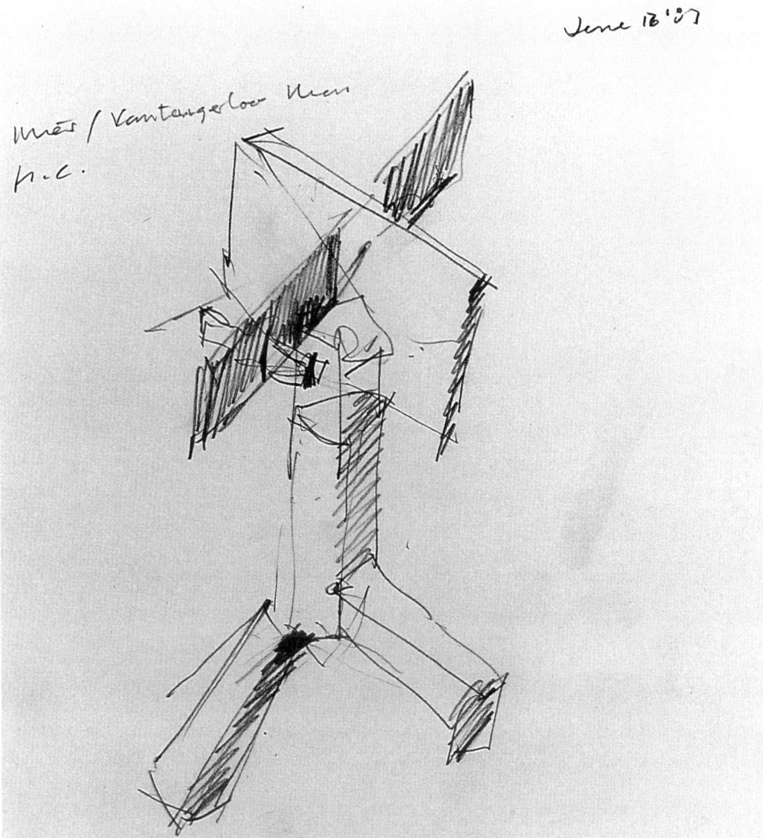

fig. 32 Melvin Charney, *Dancing De Stijl, a study of column no. 5,* 1987. Pencil on paper.

form of the church is drawn back to the Gésu in Rome, to Neolithic horned gates and symbols of passage; the arms of the spires suggest an anthropomorphic reading of the ancient composition (fig. 34). The two domed mini-temples which presently top the Sainte-Cunégonde spires, somewhat closer to God than is the congregation below, are reinterpreted on the column in the form of a house – Adam's shack in Paradise – closer to the congregation than to God.

ROW E

Column ten treats the monumental presence of the tall cylinder of a shot tower, the remains of the Stelco steel mill on rue Notre-Dame, directly south of the site.

ROW F

Column eleven is situated on the western extremity of the esplanade, directly above the expressway, on the axis of rue du Fort

fig. 33 Sainte-Cunégonde church from the west end of the esplanade. Photograph: Melvin Charney, 1987.

and the façade of the seminary of the Collège de Montréal to the north. The expressway and the seminary are united in this column. A tubular steel structure that usually supports the directional signs for the expressway now supports a façade, another "sign," similar to the pediment of the seminary. One façade is posited as the representation of the other, as elsewhere in the garden. A steel strut extends above the column to hold up a straight-back chair high above the expressway. And on the chair sits a house, the final house of the sequence of "dwellings" which began at the base of column one. This "house" is a sign of the city as a collective abode and of the essential content of a centre for architecture.

Plants

The composition of the plant material, its variety and configuration, emphasizes stratagems used in the conception of the garden: the "natural" was approached through its cultural representation. A "textual" invocation of the site and of gardens was used to unearth land and plant formations specific to the site and to correlate them to equivalent formations specific to garden architecture. Typologies were suggested; an attempt was made to distinguish indigenous species from varieties introduced into Montréal since its settlement in the seventeenth century.

Horticulture was thus generated by the formal composition of the garden. Each constituent contained a history of landform and

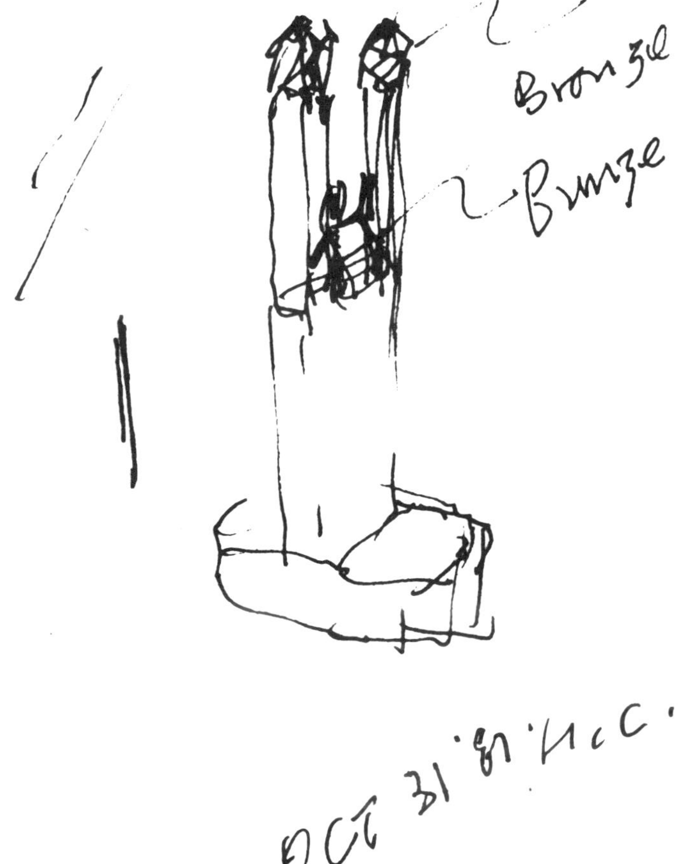

fig. 34 Melvin Charney, *Study of column no. 8,* 1987. Ink on paper.

plant material. Trees dominate. Given the nature of the site, the configuration of trees is essentially urban. There are no "woody clumps," but alignments and grids, consciously planted. Walkways are framed by rows of trees. Since the garden is located on the southern slopes of Mount Royal, considered one of the best apple-growing districts in the world in the nineteenth century (note the numerous orchards in the 1846 map of the area [fig. 21]) and part of the site itself was once an apple orchard, a grid of apple trees is planted in the garden. Similarly, the planting along the cadastral walls reflects the shrubs and flowers – prickly raspberry bushes, wild roses, sumac – which grow spontaneously along the stone walls dividing farms, and which can still be found on the island of Montréal. The landscape of rural fields was incorporated into the meadow. And the boulevard between the

garden and the CCA building was made to assume the appropriate form of a "boulevard," with a tree-lined median and sidewalks. The "appropriateness" of the planting of the boulevard, as with the other elements of the garden, is related to figural formations inherent in its existence as a type, formations readily found in Montréal.

Finally, the configuration of the planting was used to extend the boundaries of the garden to include the ramps of the expressway within its purview. Cars enter and leave the garden through a thicket of trees and shrubs as they enter and leave the city.

* * *

Thus the garden and the expressway are superposed. One is above, below, inside, and outside the other. A double presence is established. While the expressway cuts an indifferent east–west swath through the city, the garden is intertwined with the city, the mountain, and the river, north and south.

The garden transforms the site into a temporal medium. Plant materials introduce a dimension of time – the cycle of the seasons, decay and generation – while some of the formal elements recognize previous states of the site, and the columns suggest the transience of things. The purpose is not to celebrate the past, but to expose the place in the present, as a singular fragment of the city, and as an ongoing process of transformation whose most recent embodiment is that of a garden.

A garden by its very nature tends to evoke old, stereotypical images of a lost Arcadia. This garden is situated on an expressway that is no more than a place of lost urbanity, a lost city. And if Paradise is a garden at one end of time and a city at the other, somewhere outside the world, as the underpinnings of tradition would have it, then either all is lost or we are now outside history in a world in which new relationships can be forged only out of an amalgam of elusive metaphors, be they a garden or a city.

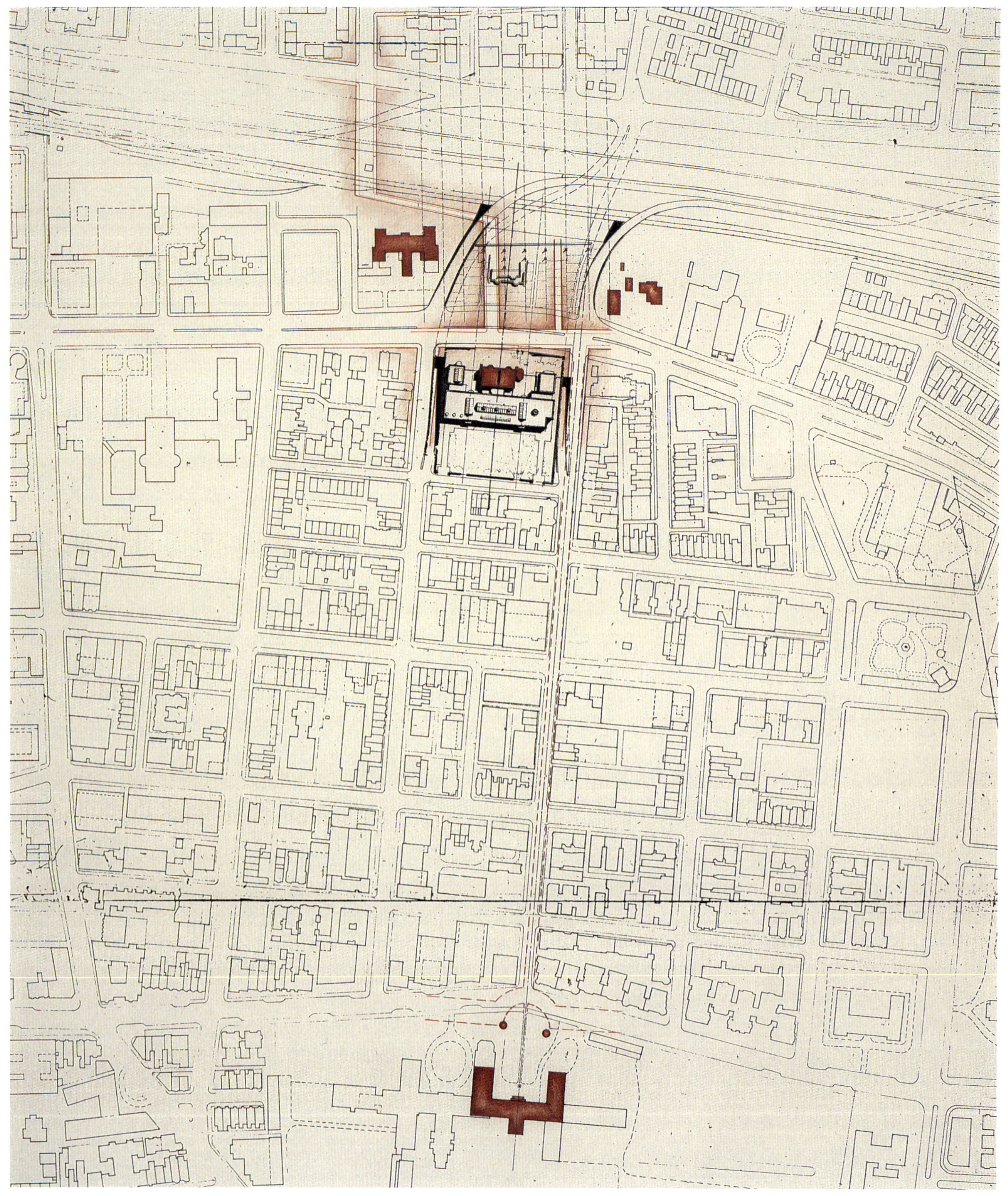

fig. 36 Melvin Charney, *Plan of the CCA Garden*, 1988. Coloured pencil and ink on vellum.

fig. 35 Melvin Charney, *The two intersecting sets of urban axes of the CCA Garden and the layers of the site*, 1987. Coloured pencil and ink on vellum. Note, in red, rue des Seigneurs, which traversed the site, and buildings dating from the mid-nineteenth century.

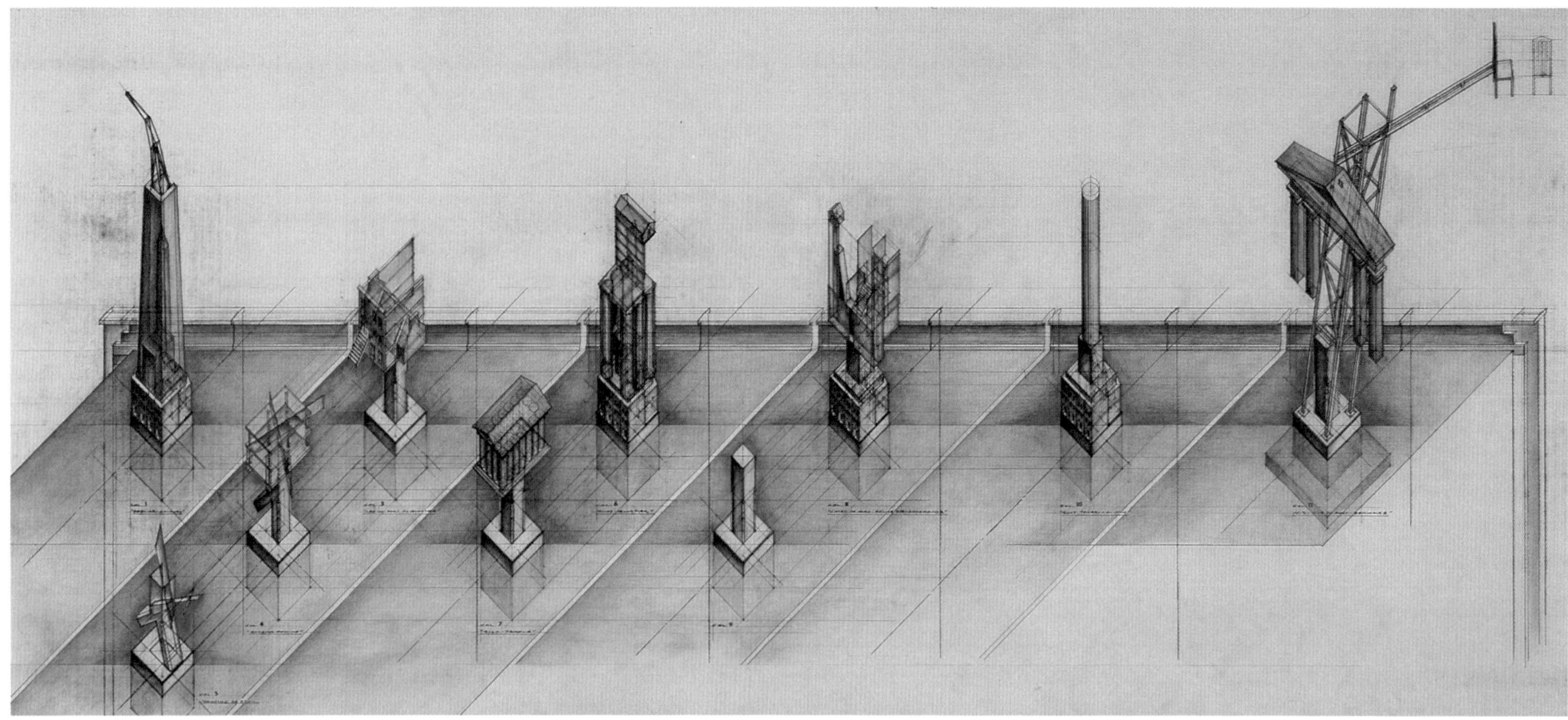

fig. 37 Melvin Charney, *The allegorical columns of the CCA Garden,* 1988. Coloured pencil and ink on vellum.

Portfolio 3

Photographs by Richard Pare
and Gabor Szilasi
December 1987 – January 1989

Partial view of the south elevation at the Shaughnessy House. Photograph: Gabor Szilasi, January 1989.

Partial view of the north elevation at the centre line. Photograph: Richard Pare, November 1988.

Entrance Court details. Photograph: Richard Pare, January 1989.

View of the Entrance Court and West Rotunda, looking south. Photograph: Richard Pare, January 1989.

View of Special Collections Study Room and scholars' offices, looking northeast. Photograph: Richard Pare, November 1988.

Partial view of south elevation and Scholars' Wing with cornice under construction. Photograph: Richard Pare, November 1988.

View of Library Court and reading rooms, looking northeast. Photograph: Gabor Szilasi, January 1989.

The long galleries. Photograph: Gabor Szilasi, January 1989.

Partial view of offices, curatorial level. Photograph: Gabor Szilasi, December 1988.

Southeast corner of the exhibitions work space, curatorial level, showing partially glazed interior window. Photograph: Gabor Szilasi, December 1987.

Corridor, collections vault level. Photograph: Gabor Szilasi, November 1988.

Compact storage shelving in archives vault. Photograph: Gabor Szilasi, December 1988.

CCA Garden and south window reflected in glazed north wall of Scholars' Wing.
Photograph: Richard Pare, November 1988.

Fenestration study. Photograph: Gabor Szilasi, December 1988.

View of south elevation showing Shaughnessy House and Scholars' Wing, looking east. Photograph: Gabor Szilasi, January 1989.

fig. 38 Composite aerial view of the CCA building and site from the west.
Photomontage: Gabor Szilasi, 1988.

Critical Classicism and the Restoration of Architectural Consciousness

LARRY RICHARDS

When seen from above, the Canadian Centre for Architecture looks like a three-dimensional E (fig. 38). A closer examination shifts one's perception because the middle leg of the E is distinctive; the figure begins to appear as a C, trying to pull away from but symmetrically embracing a smaller-scaled, more intricate piece. The chiselled geometries and decisive locking into the ground give the impression that these forms have existed in this arrangement for many years. A picture of order emerges.

One of the boldest elements of the whole is the long, north-facing façade of the primary CCA volume – the straight edge of the E. It makes the fourth side of an urban square, the other three sides of the rectangular open space being formed predominantly by the fronts of consecutive townhouses. And at the heart of the square a precisely defined park recalls similar places of calm in the fabric of nineteenth-century Montréal.

One's attention is then drawn south to a second major open space in the composition: a garden which is topographically more complex and more architecturally agitated than the quiet, flat park to the north. The garden slopes up from the CCA buildings, terminating with an esplanade overlooking the industrial *quartier* below and the St. Lawrence River and Mount Saint-Hilaire beyond. Marked by a "forest" of abstract, allegorical columns, the landscape is much grander at this point – expansive, searching, intentionally less sure of limits. In contrast with the inward-focused park, so elegantly bound by aluminum fences, the garden opens outward, accepting and engaging in the uncertainties of the late twentieth-century city.

fig. 39 The Saidye Bronfman Centre on côte Sainte-Catherine, Montréal. Phyllis Lambert, architect, 1963–68. Photograph: Richard Nickel, 1968. Courtesy of the Richard Nickel Committee.

This willingness to engage in uncertainty is underscored by a relatively small but important construction, situated down the slope. Directly opposite the ornate Shaughnessy House, a portion of the mansion has been reconstructed to mirror its Victorian façade. The doubling is an example of one of the formal preoccupations which informed the urban, architectural, and landscape design of the CCA: a rigorous and complex setting up of bilateral symmetries which are subsequently subverted, transformed and reassimilated. A reflexive device which generates a zone of disturbance between the mansion and its double, this fragment is profound in its simultaneous act of balancing / stabilizing and unbalancing / destabilizing. The fragment can be read as a second, "new mansion" under construction, or an identical "old mansion" in a state of ruin; the fragment momentarily reveals the Shaughnessy House in its previous state *without* the new building wrapped around it, inviting one to visually construct the ghost of the reversed C; and since any visitor to the garden can occupy the house-as-folly and look across to the institutionalized, real Shaughnessy House, notions of private and public domain become (intentionally) conceptually

confused. The tension between the Shaughnessy House and its mirror-image commands us to confront our individual and collective memory of Montréal and, beyond the city, life's universal cycle of construction and destruction.

However, this initial intoxication with the landscape – with a kind of preordained essentiality and familiarity – becomes difficult to sustain because, down there, several less beautiful aspects of the modern metropolis curiously bracket and thread through the CCA precinct, juxtaposing random speed and noise with the willful architectural oasis. Two of the edges contain expressway ramps, and a wide boulevard cuts through the middle. Green and white expressway signs, harsh lighting, and brutal concrete retaining walls announce that traffic engineers have left their marks, threatening the continuity and traditions of the public realm. Walter Benjamin's statement that "Memory is the complement of experience lived," is apropos in this context since this bird's-eye view of the landscape of the Canadian Centre for Architecture invites readings which fluctuate between an imagined orderly past and a real, fragmented present into which are nested new fragments of order.[1]

Within this matrix, the CCA park and garden are havens, alternatives to the capsulated, asphalt-dominated world of the private automobile. Quietly, a lesson in urbanity is presented, and with it an institution's belief that it is possible and necessary to restore architectural consciousness, if only as a polemical fragment, in the midst of the modern rush.

* * *

The three parts which appear so clearly from above – the building, park, and garden – are the largest-scaled components of an essentially classical composition. The specific use of formal devices in the creation of the CCA will be assessed; but the more general progenitors of the underlying classical order deserve attention first. These can be traced to an intersection of the architectural backgrounds and obsessions of the two primary designers of the centre: Peter Rose, the architect, and Phyllis Lambert, the consulting architect.

fig. 40 Rally in front of the Shaughnessy House in 1973, protesting the demolition of historic buildings in Montréal. Photograph: Pierre McCann, *La Presse*, 1974.

Phyllis Lambert's classical predilections informed the defining, designing and building of the CCA over a twelve-year period. Her knowledge and application of classical principles have come full circle: from early familiarity with the classically based greystone architecture of Montréal, to studies and work in the 1950s and 1960s with Mies van der Rohe in the United States, to her design for the Miesian Saidye Bronfman Centre in Montréal (fig. 39), to the realization, finally, of a Montréal greystone building for the CCA. In a project meeting in August 1984, Lambert expressed her "affinity for quietness [and] simplicity" and her "tendency towards the classical." Most revealing is her statement, in the context of discussions about the classical tradition and greystone building in Montréal, that "It is something in one's bones … solutions come out of what one has always known."

Lambert was instrumental in arranging a 1983 exhibition at the Musée des beaux-arts in Montréal, "The Villas of Pliny and Classical Architecture in Montréal." It included material loaned by the Institut Français d'Architecture (from its 1982 Paris exhibition "La Laurentine et l'invention de la villa Romaine" which Lambert saw and admired), as well as additional historical items relating to Montréal. The installation included a contemporary construction by Melvin Charney which helped to integrate the viewers' experience of the 125 works of art. The highly acclaimed exhibition can

be seen as a manifestation of Phyllis Lambert's desire to provide opportunities for the public to understand certain threads of Montréal architecture more deeply – to reveal the historical continuity and transformational power of the classical tradition.

More than a decade before the Pliny exhibition, Lambert and other Montréalers became determined to confront the wanton destruction of the city's fabric through misguided development and superficial design. Not only were historic buildings of value coming down, but entire neighbourhoods were being devastated through the careless insertion of inappropriate building types or simply by the proliferation of weed-filled, desolate lots. The city seemed bent on erasing its own history. This returns us to the elaborate centre leg of the E, the 1874 Shaughnessy House, which was one of many buildings threatened with demolition in the early 1970s (fig. 40). Lambert acquired and saved the building in 1974, and it became a generative artifact for the CCA design. Its restoration has subsequently been integral to the rehabilitation of the neighbourhood.

Although the Shaughnessy House is French Second Empire in style, it is more important to focus on its classical, bilaterally symmetrical composition because the regulating lines of the new building, the C, derive from it. Although generally understood by the public to be a single dwelling – a mansion – the Shaughnessy House was actually constructed as two adjacent houses. Designed by William T. Thomas, the west one was owned and occupied by Duncan McIntyre and the east one by Robert Brown. Thomas G. Shaughnessy purchased the east house in 1892 and lived there until 1923, adding rooms and making modifications over the years which included additions and alterations by the prominent Montréal architect Edward Maxwell. Lord Strathcona, who lived in the mansion that stood to the west at the corner of bouvelard René-Lévesque and rue du Fort bought the west house in 1895 and used it as his family's guest house until 1927. In 1901, Strathcona constructed an enclosed passage between his mansion's greenhouse and the conservatory of the Shaughnessy House, as it came to be known, thus making an unusual "train" of three houses which were being used in a manner very different from their architectural presentation to the Montréal public (fig. 41). In 1945, when the two Shaughnessy houses were consolidated by the Sisters of Service as one institutional building, the

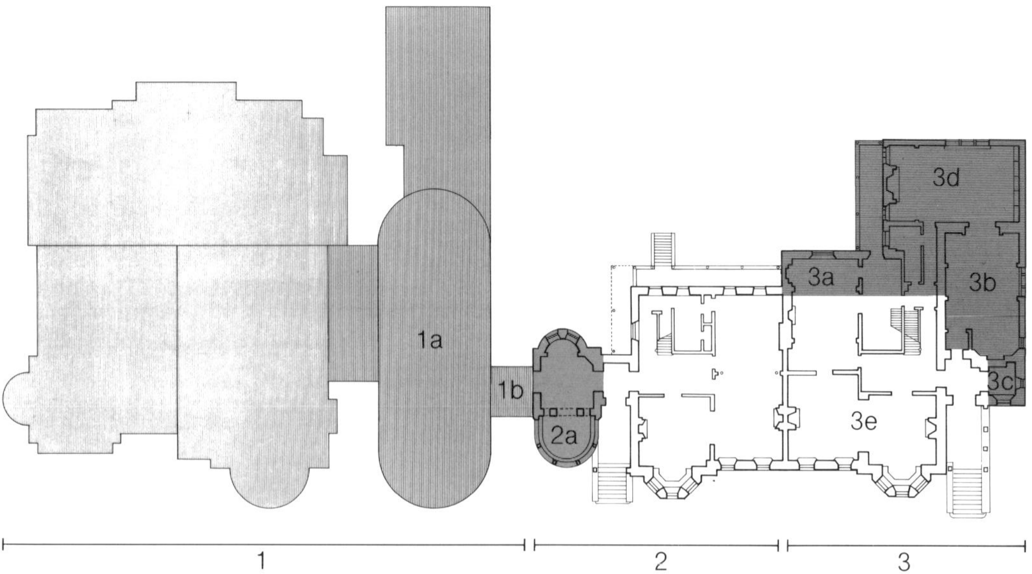

1   Lord Strathcona's house 1886–87, Hutchison and Steele, architects
1a Strathcona House conservatory 1886–87, Hutchison and Steele, architects
1b Conservatories linked 1900, Edward Maxwell, architect

2   Duncan McIntyre's house 1874–75, William T. Thomas, architect.
2a Conservatory added ca. 1885, architect unknown

3   Robert Brown's house 1874–75, William T. Thomas, architect, showing changes 1897, 1907
3a Dining room extended 1897, Edward Maxwell, architect
3b Billiard room added 1897, Edward Maxwell, architect
3c Cloakroom added 1897, Edward Maxwell, architect
3d Library added 1907, Finley and Spence, architects
3e Drawing room renovated 1907, Finley and Spence, architects

fig. 41 Main floor plan of the Shaughnessy House, showing changes 1886–1907. Drawing: David Kepron, office of Peter Rose Architect, 1988.

new owners had the centre mitoyen wall broken through so that they could reorganize the relationship of rooms to serve their needs. The centre wall that had separated the two houses for seventy years finally became a *binding* rather than a *dividing* element. So when Lambert acquired the Shaughnessy House it already had a history of complexity and contradiction, and it was to generate more. In 1983, Peter Rose, who had made various proposals for the building since 1979, was appointed architect for the new CCA building. Referring to the house as "a weird biaxial scheme with nothing but a rain gutter at the centre," Rose likes to reflect on the fact that in later years the building "had two entries but only one was used," because the west half was Lord Strathcona's guest house, bizarrely linked to his family's residence. For Lambert and Rose, the latent energies of the Shaughnessy House were to become active, instrumental agents in the process of designing the new CCA building.

Following a series of studies by Barton Myers Associates (with Rose and Peter Lanken as consulting architects) in late 1980 and early 1981 whose aim was to accommodate the CCA in a renovated 1948 Hudson's Bay Company warehouse in the heart of downtown Montréal, Phyllis Lambert became more interested in the

Shaughnessy House and in Montréal greystone buildings. She decided to design the new Canadian Centre for Architecture herself, working with her Los Angeles-based firm, Ridgway. Collaborating with Gene Summers, she refocused on the quirky mansion, which was boarded up and surrounded with weeds. In the spring of 1981 the Quebec City firm of restoration architects, Bilodeau St-Louis, completed their report, "Maison Shaughnessy Montréal, Québec – Rapport d'entretien: architecture mécanique et structure." During August 1981, Ridgway produced three designs for the Shaughnessy House site. Recorded in a September 1981 document titled "Programme et développement du site préliminaire," alternatives A and B include schematic site plans and photographs of massing models (figs. 42, 43). Alternative C, which eventually became the preferred direction, includes schematic floor plans in addition to the site plan and massing model (figs. 44, 45). The three designs share certain characteristics, and it is obvious that the same classically inspired eyes and hands are at work in all three. There was an attempt in every case to keep new building volumes as far away from the mansion as possible.

In A, a long, simple rectangular volume is placed along the north edge of the site, tight to rue Baile and linked underground to the Shaughnessy House. The proposed new building is essentially

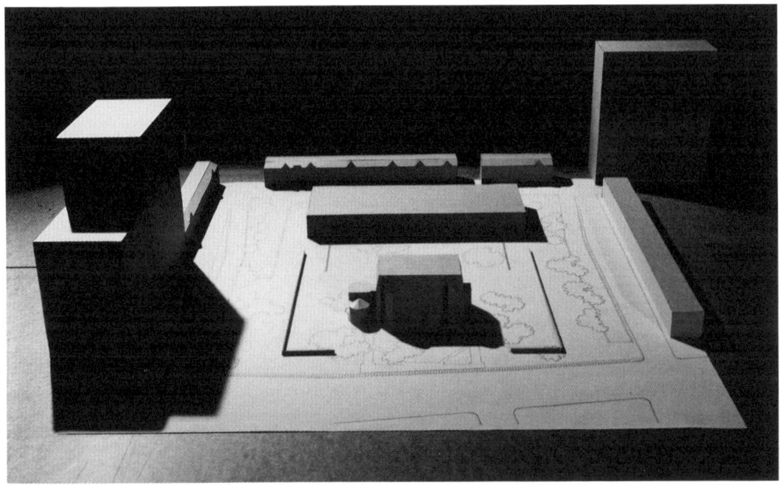

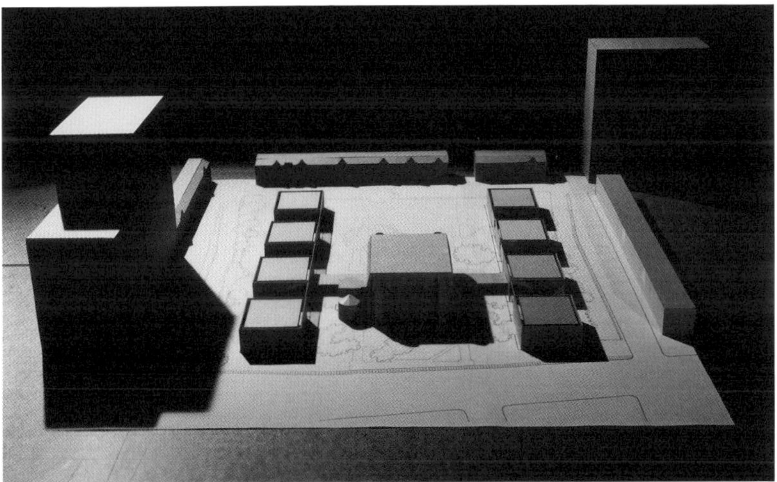

figs. 42–44 Massing models A, B, and C. Ridgway Inc. for the CCA. Reproduced from "Programme et développement de site préliminaire," CCA, 1981. These studies show relationships between the new building and the Shaughnessy House.

Miesian with four cruciform columns supporting an upper mass; space flows underneath. This proposal can be seen as two opposing villas set in an extensive garden: one modern, the other Victorian; but both classically based. In B, the house is mirror-imaged to the north and then linked by enclosed passageways to a series of four square pavilions along both the east and west edges of the site. This forms an H-shaped composition which generates a small garden between the Shaughnessy House and boulevard René-Lévesque and a large, square garden between the house and rue Baile. B places the exhibition space underground; study rooms and other research facilities needing natural light are disposed in the eight pavilions. Alternative C shows the house mirror-imaged to the north again, but in a more explicit manner than B. Quite boldly, all of the other new space is pushed below grade. Eight large skylights / lanterns protrude from underground, each in approximately the same location as the pavilions in B. The radical attempt in C to improve circulation and communication within the new space and between the new space and the mansion allowed Lambert to achieve the possibility, partially tested in alternative A, whereby the Shaughnessy House is left alone as a villa in a garden.

Somewhat ironically, after abandoning the Hudson's Bay warehouse project to turn her attention to the Shaughnessy House site, Lambert was confronted with the architectural difficulty of adding to it. As she was to comment nearly six years later, "I was scared to touch it [the Shaughnessy House]." She had not yet found a way to reconcile her interests in antiquity, in the principles of Mies van der Rohe, and in classical greystone Montréal. Essentially these varying interests emerged as tensions between the reductive and structuralist on the one hand, and the more inclusive and emblematic on the other.

Beyond these fundamental conceptual and aesthetic struggles, careful thought was already being given to environmental concerns such as the desirability and difficulty of having abundant natural light in an institution of this kind at a northern latitude. The Ridgway schemes of 1981 also acknowledged thermal considerations; for example, the advantages of simple shapes and volumes were stressed and even the extreme of going almost entirely underground to fully protect the predominantly paper collections

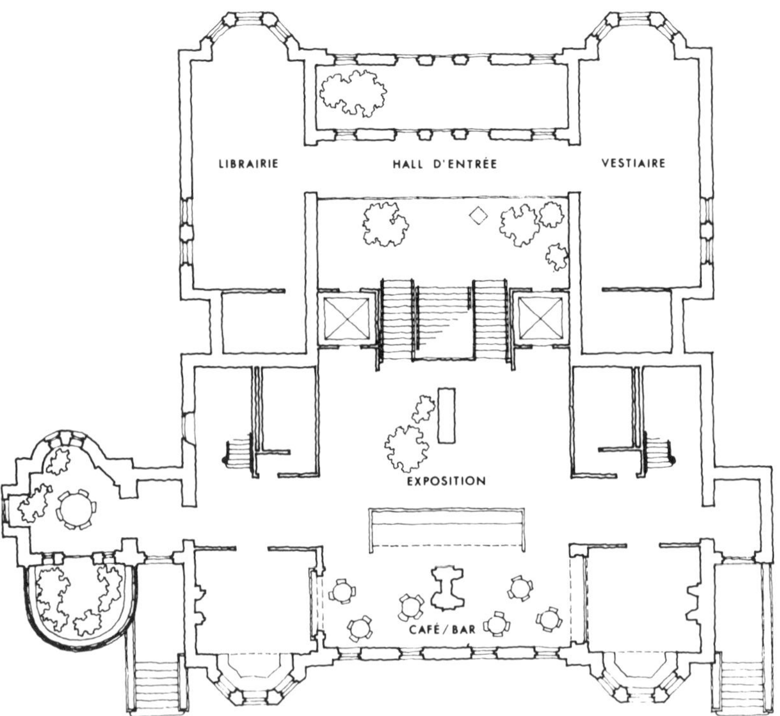

fig. 45 Main floor plan study in alternative C for additions to the Shaughnessy House. Ridgway Inc. for the CCA. Reproduced from "Programme et developpement du site preliminaire," CCA, 1981.

was considered. (It is interesting to note that the underground schemes led to a final decision to place the extensive storage vaults below grade. Eventually there were two primary reasons for placing two levels of storage space underground: for protection, and to keep the centre low and in scale with nearby buildings. Toward the end of the design process, the architects began to see the below-grade vaults as the symbolic base of the institution; that is, the collections themselves are the CCA "foundations.") And always, unyieldingly, the Ridgway designs are symmetrical about an axis running through the centre wall of the Shaughnessy House and in response to the original north–south property lines defining *cadastre* number 1630.

Although the Ridgway schemes preceded the final Peter Rose *parti* by more than two years, it is clear that these studies indirectly influenced later work through Lambert's role as consulting architect. A suggests the possibility of a large, rectangular building across the site; B shows pavilions to each side of the Shaughnessy House; and C makes a case for underground adjacencies, dramatic top lighting, and an urban square defined by the existing townhouses. The long, east–west corridors and adjacent service spaces of the realized centre can also be traced back to the Ridgway designs.

Lambert recommended the further development of alternative C, the only one of the Ridgway alternatives to include floor plans. In the September 1981 report we see, for the first time, a café and bar in the Shaughnessy House, along with administrative offices. The proposed new areas are to be built in two phases: phase one, adjacent to the Shaughnessy House, has conservation laboratories, book preservation rooms, and a large vault for the collections; phase two more than doubles the size of the collections storage vaults and adds wings to the east and west of the mansion – one for exhibitions and the other for an auditorium. The location of these wings is nearly the same as the built wings which now bracket the house. The primary approach to the institution in C is from the north (rue Baile) side. At the mid-point of a new volume, which is the mirror-image of the Shaughnessy House, a grand stair is shown. This central entrance and stair notion perplexed the designers for a long time, and one suspects that the element generating the formal resistance to entering on the centre line was the dictatorial middle wall of the house. Also, entering on the central axis of a composition means that one must choose between left and right, splitting the experience. Lambert soon realized that the integrated nature of the CCA collections and her desire for visitors to gain a sense of the institution as a whole could not support a central entry scheme.

In all three schemes, the Maxwell-designed billiard room and the library have been removed from the east side of the Shaughnessy House. Presumably this was done for four reasons: the addition lacked architectural coherence; it was a maze (in Lambert's words, "a rabbit warren"); it undermined the mansion as a free-standing object; and it caused great difficulty in adding rationally to the house. However, this removal can also be read as a demand for bilateral symmetry, for a perfect, complete whole.

In one of the subsequent Ridgway designs, the Maxwell rooms are replaced by a rather imposing circular stair hall (figs. 46, 47). The stair element, in certain ways balancing and relating to the very elegant conservatory on the southwest corner, was capped by a cone, and the entire volume was to be glazed. This cylinder was aggressively modern, accommodating a system of steps and ramps on the interior and around the outer edges which took visitors from boulevard René-Lévesque to one of three destinations: the Shaughnessy House; the lower, new floors; or the gardens behind the house. As well, there was an elevator at the centre. In retrospect, the design for this circular stair piece stands as a reminder of attempts to resolve the question of entry and of front and back on the site. The Shaughnessy House announced itself – fronted – on boulevard René-Levesque; but the expansion necessitated a new entrance because the domestic scale of the house could not accommodate large groups of visitors. Clearly this proposal for a major cylindrical element (placed asymmetrically to the east) did something important: it demonstrated that it was not imperative to enter the new composition on the central axis, something which Peter Rose and his design team later confronted and resolved. In fact, the realized entry bay facing rue Baile, in its placement and transparency, can be seen as a "flip" – a compositional reversal and transformation of the earlier glazed cylinder.

The plans for the Ridgway scheme, drawn in the spring of 1983, are precise, and show the long east–west corridor and treasure wall which, from that point forward, remained in all of the designs. The main exhibition and reading rooms are still underground, symmetrically positioned on either side of Lambert's pro-posal for a thick-walled central room with a flat-domed ceiling (fig. 48). In a diagram of this room by Summers, complete with niches, a more articulated classical language begins to emerge (fig. 49). The generating lines and the framework start to be populated by specific configurations – an order that goes through many transformations, eventually permeating the entire new building. The flexible, universal space of Mies van der Rohe, which was celebrated in the earlier Ridgway schemes, seems far away.

Looking back, Lambert says she began to realize that she was determined to create a masonry building for the CCA, but "didn't know how" in relation to the Shaughnessy House and thus kept pushing everything underground. At the same time she knew that "a Montréal greystone building was essential," and she was beginning to reconnect with her masonry training from Mies (himself a mason's son). Several years later, reflecting on the construction of the CCA, she said: "Having been trained by Mies, I can tell you how to construct a stone corner … I know from Mies, always lay stone horizontally, as it is in the earth." Late in 1983, she made the major decision to appoint Peter Rose architect for the new CCA building and the Shaughnessy House renovations. Erol Argun was assigned associate architect for the project, Bilodeau St-Louis were engaged as the restoration architects, and Phyllis Lambert was the consulting architect.

On the choice of Peter Rose, Phyllis Lambert says, "Peter and I have walked and walked together and looked at buildings in Montréal … Although I had done the earlier work, it has always been Peter's building; but I had confidence that I could direct it … The Rose scheme comes more from the problem and the situation at hand, rather than from the Ridgway scheme." One could also say that the Shaughnessy House was the problem and Montréal the situation at hand, and Peter Rose was quite ready to touch both. He quickly absorbed Lambert's studies for the Shaughnessy House site and a close working relationship between the two architects evolved. Denis St-Louis, architect for the restoration, had a lower profile but must be seen as an essential contributor throughout the design and construction phases, since the Shaughnessy House is the set piece, the heart of the CCA composition.

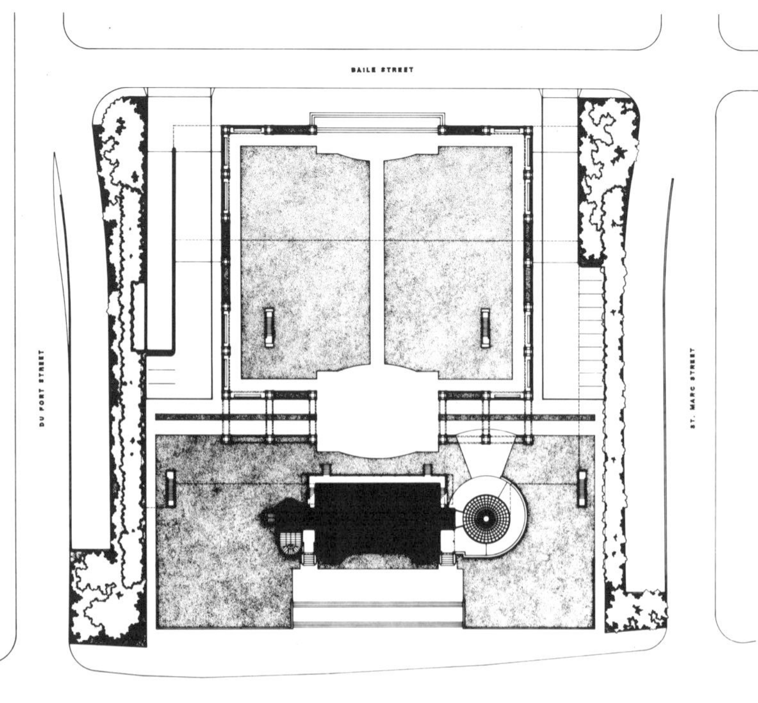

fig. 46 Site plan study for underground additions to the Shaughnessy House. Ridgway Inc. for the CCA, 1983. CCA (AR1985:0002:0001).

Educated at Yale University and strongly influenced by Charles Moore, dean of the Yale School of Architecture from 1965 to 1971, Peter Rose was well known in Canada by the late 1970s. His knowledge and use of history and tradition, sometimes with an ironic twist, gained full expression in a series of spirited houses and small buildings in Quebec which were regionalist in the best sense of emerging from local conventions and traditions. By the time Lambert appointed him architect for the CCA, Rose was also identified by his increasingly classical position, exemplified by the inclusion of his Ski Pavilion Soixante-Dix at Saint-Sauveur, Quebec (1977) in the 1980 publication, *Post-Modern Classicism: The New Synthesis* (guest-edited by Charles Jencks). In fact, Rose was the only Canadian included in the book. Even more revealing of his architectural obsessions a decade ago is an article he co-authored called "Montreal: Ten Buildings to See" (1981). Rose's choice of the ten monumental works which he considered the most significant architecture in the city included three built in the nineteenth century and seven from before 1940; in other words, there were *no* contemporary works in the selection.

For example, Rose presents us with the Jacques Cartier Bridge (1925–28): "From a distance the pavilion-like structure resembles a giant white fortress." Of the Royal Bank of Canada, a twenty-storey building faced with Ontario and Quebec limestone (1926–28), he writes: "The interior plan also reflects the palazzo prototype. Enter through the revolving doors on rue St. Jacques, and ascend the triumphal staircase to one of the most magnificent banking halls in the country." He describes the Aldred Building (1921–31): "the Indiana limestone building is buttressed and set back at the eighth, thirteenth and sixteenth floors. The strong verticality of the building is further accentuated by the use of decorative cast aluminum spandrels." Of Mount Royal Cemeteries (1852–1900s), he says : "With their flowering trees, hedges and gardens these cemeteries can be considered the first urban parks in the city, predating Frederick Law Olmsted's Mount Royal Park by twenty years. Early tourist guides and Montreal postcards drew attention to them, focusing on the picturesque stone entrance gateways and the beauty and variety of monuments contained within." [2]

Six of Rose's favourite structures were built predominantly of stone. In "Montréal: Ten Buildings to See," there is almost a prediction of what Montréal's eleventh building to see would be eight years later. *Trace* editor George Baird states in his introduction to the article:

Is it too much then, to speculate that this itinerary is both archeological and psychological? May I suggest that Leggatt, Lemire and Rose's list, in its infamiliarity, in its route from water to mountain, in its symbolic preoccupations, is a revelation of a secret architecture of Montréal, or for that matter, a glimpse of some as yet only partially grasped potential Canadianness in architecture, sui generis?" [3]

Although "Montréal: Ten Buildings to See" adds considerable insight to our understanding of some of the Montréal influences on Rose's work, others came to bear and deserve mention. For many years before commencing work on the CCA, he undertook a thorough study of the work of Schinkel, Lutyens, Cormier, Kahn, Scarpa, of McKim, Mead and White, and of Shaker builders, learning in particular about manipulation of light and use of substantial materials such as stone. In 1984, the addition to Rose's staff of two Princeton graduates who had studied under Michael Graves propelled the office's already well-developed interests in

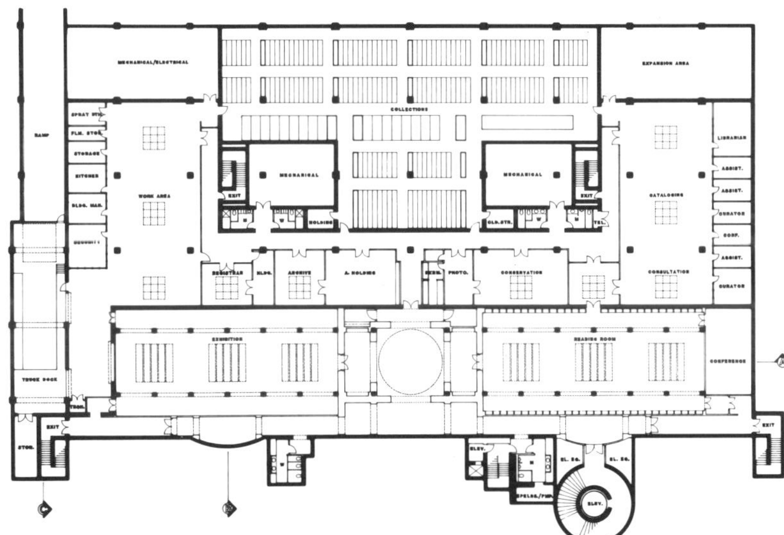

fig. 47 Model of site plan study for underground additions to the Shaughnessy House. Ridgway Inc. for the CCA, 1983.

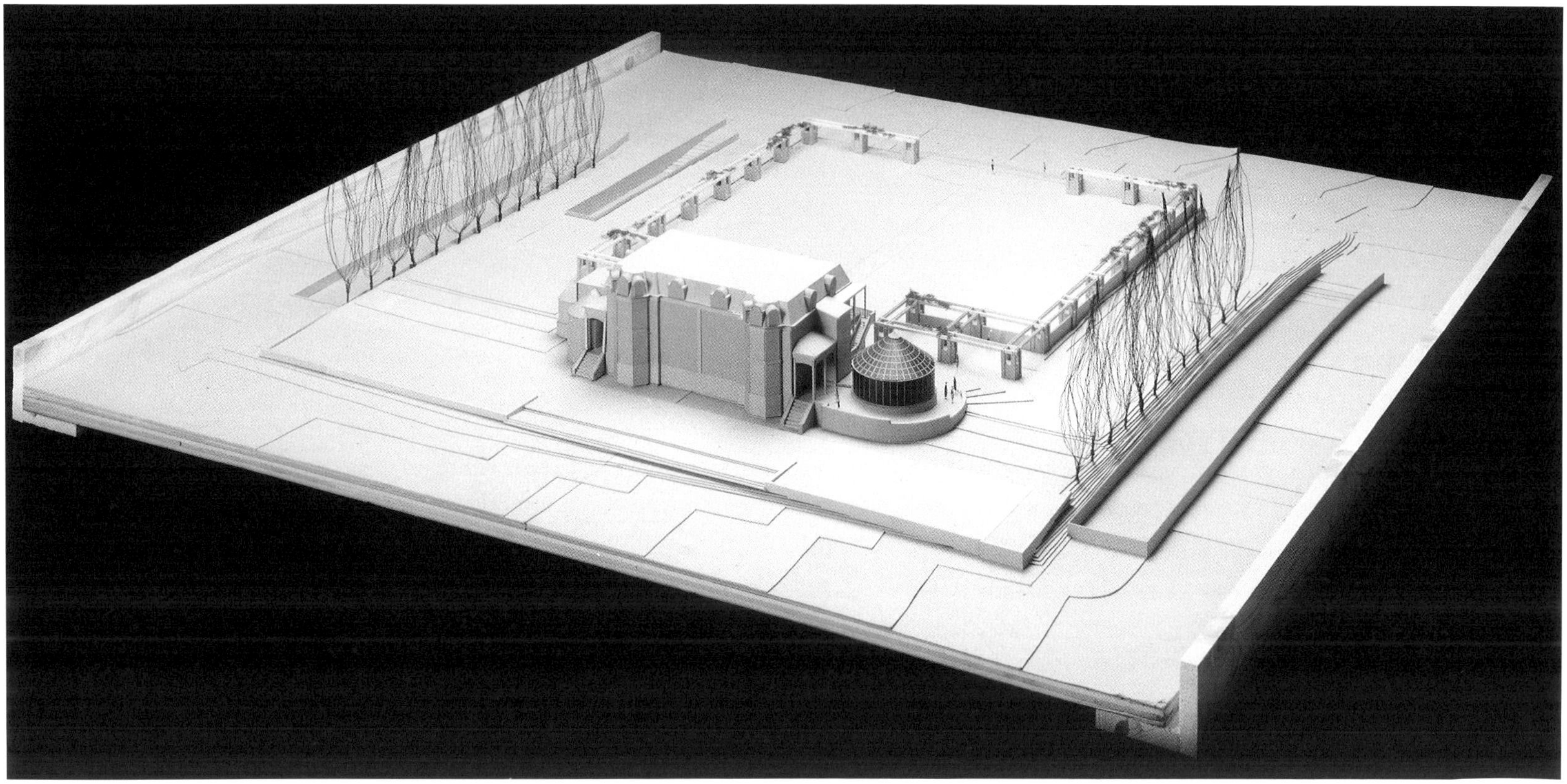

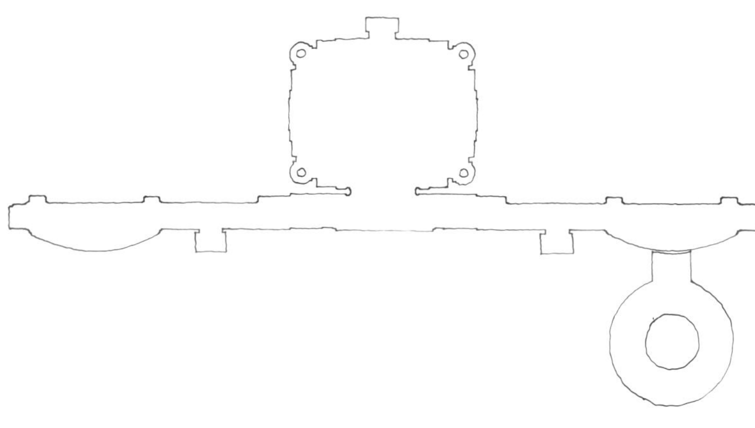

fig. 48 Main floor plan study for underground addition to the Shaughnessy House. Ridgway Inc. for the CCA, 1983. CCA (AR1985:0002:0002).

fig. 49 Diagram of circulation, underground addition to Shaughnessy House. Ridgway Inc. for the CCA, 1983. CCA (AR1985:0002:0003).

colour and ornament even further. One can feel Graves in the background in a series of experiments with the CCA project during 1984 (figs. 50, 51). These studies, many of them for the north, rue Baile façade, were exuberant. However, happily, the completed building has few vestiges of Gravesian indulgences; aluminum and light in the right proportions and shapes can sustain interest longer than the kinds of dolphin and swan flourishes which have come to undermine the classical strengths of Graves's work.

Finally, it is fair to say that in the late stages of the CCA design process, Peter Rose became more interested in industrial, manufactured building components; in tough materials that age gracefully; and in a more abstract sense of ornament. This seems to have happened for several reasons, chief among them his exposure to work in Vienna (Wagner), Italy (Rossi), and new work in California (Morphosis' Mayne and Rotondi). Rose's work began to change considerably as part of the general North American revival of interest in modernism, and the parts of the CCA which were designed last (such as the auditorium interior and the library tables detailed in 1988) reflect the transition in his thinking. The evolution of Rose's work from 1983 to 1988 must also be assessed in the context of his collaboration with Lambert.

The Canadian Centre for Architecture, in its contrasting weighty stone and light-reflective metal fittings, embodies a Canadianness and Quebecness; and, as George Baird pondered, this makes one wonder more about the sources of a "secret architecture in Montréal." The source is surely deeply embedded in the place, in nature, in the earth. It is at the moment when an enormous stone is lifted from its bed that part of the secret is given away. Gravity is resisted, saw blades cut, and the geometricized pieces are moved to new places of stasis and authority. But the shape is particular to a place and time, to the imagination and will of the architect. And to complicate matters, in the case of the CCA the architects themselves have been shaped by that Quebec environment. Rose and Lambert rediscovered what Montréal's early builders naturally understood: the Quebec landscape offers its greystone for cutting and shaping in response to the technological possibilities and the aesthetics of the time. Significantly for the outcome of the CCA, their aesthetic was essentially classical.

fig. 50 Study for the Scholars' Wing. Drawing: Erik Marosi, office of Peter Rose Architect, 1984.

As natives of Montréal, Lambert and Rose retain their belief in what this tradition represents socially and politically as well as aesthetically.

Although it is not within the scope of this essay, nor in the province of this author, to assess the classical order of the CCA building and site in depth, it does seem useful to examine briefly the system of hierarchical composition which permeates the whole and which is revealed in the site plan and in the plans, sections, and elevations of the building (see pages 79–86). The canonic system of classicism – the three layers of formal devices – is summarized by Alexander Tzonis and Liane Lefaivre as "(1) *Taxis* [from Aristotle], which divides architectural works into parts; (2) *genera*, the individual elements that populate the parts as divided by taxis; and (3) *symmetry,* the relations between individual elements."[4] Taxis and symmetry (particularly tripartition or beginning, middle, and end) are aggressively operative in the CCA. However, the genera, the architectural elements which populate the framework established by taxis and which are normally *the* classical orders, are radically transformed. In the CCA we find no Tuscan, Doric, Ionic, Corinthian, or Composite systems; rather, a highly abstracted functionalist and constructional order is embedded as intellectual, minimal "genera." Materiality and proportions are stressed. Only when we consider such elements as the stone

fig. 51 Study for the north elevation. Drawing: Nick Garrison, office of Peter Rose Architect, 1984.

bullnose and the overall profile constituting the base coursing, or experience the light filtering through the projecting aluminum cornice, do we recall the formal layer of the genera. Ornament, as part of genera, is extremely reductive in the new CCA building, limited to such elements as the rhythmic stainless-steel inserts which pin back the uppermost stone panels and, collectively, suggest a classical frieze. But, at the moment when this registers, one recalls that in classical architecture the cornice is above the frieze, not below it as Rose has executed it for the CCA. Or is the CCA "frieze" understood to be the complex patterns of light and shadow cast by the modern aluminum cornice (see page 105)?

In terms of taxis, the centre line of the CCA composition is the most important (fig. 52). It originated with the property line – the bisection of *cadastre* number 1630 – on which the separating wall between the two houses was built, a line which gains expression in the new building as a row of structural columns. Three of these columns are freestanding in the new building and are individually and hierarchically articulated (concrete, concrete and stone, stone) to represent the progression from the Shaughnessy House passage / link (a subjugated volume) to the major galleries, which are the spaces of the institution where work and public meet. This regulating centre line "breaks through" the rue Baile façade as a subtle vertical in the stone cladding – a reflection, in Peter Rose's

words, of the Shaughnessy House "zipper" (see page 104). The centre line continues through the park to the north and the garden to the south, informing the landscape design. Along rue Baile where the controlling line intersects the aluminum fence, the direction of the L-shaped "pickets" reverses east and west to acknowledge the presence of the order at this outer boundary of the property. Across the boulevard, the line shifts and reappears as a fragment in the garden by architect and artist Melvin Charney. In one of his constructions, the mirrored Shaughnessy House, he brings to the public a memory of the centre wall and the original property division. With some imagination one can infinitely extend the line through the mountain … across the river … around the world.

Secondary, symmetrically placed axes establish the Entrance Court to the west and the Library Court to the east. A third pair of axes control the positioning of the auditorium wing and the special collections wing, which flank the Shaughnessy House. These tertiary axes are symmetrical in the rue Baile façade, since each locates the centre window in the outer sets of three, determining the centre line of the major spaces in these areas (library to the east; bookstore to the west). The axes then continue into

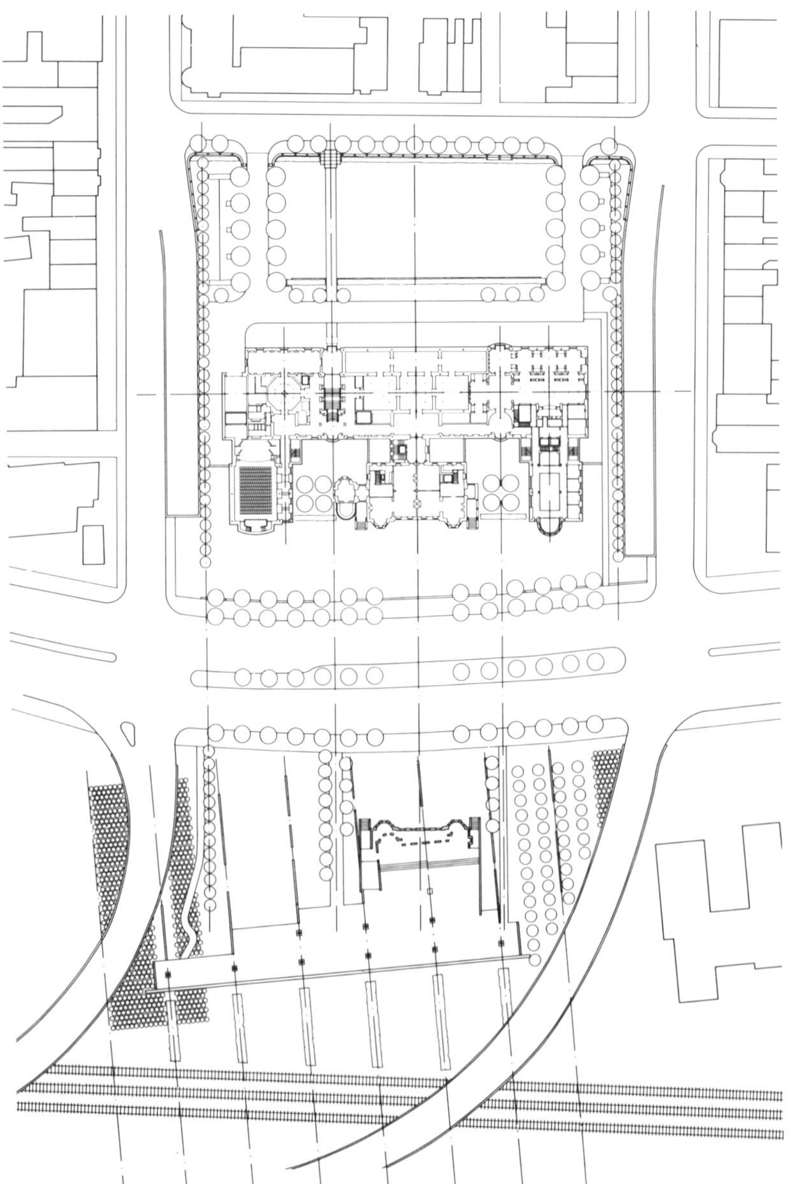

fig. 52 Site plan of the CCA including the the CCA Garden. Drawing: Jill Alexander, office of Peter Rose Architect, 1988. The drawing, at the public level, shows axial organization.

the wings flanking the mansion, the one to the east marking the centre of the Special Collections Study Room and the one to the west marking the centre of the stepped loggia adjacent to the auditorium. It becomes apparent at this point that sophisticated adjustments have been made between taxis and symmetry, but any nervousness that we might feel about actual loss of order is temporary, for the conflicts and violations are soon reconciled. For example, a void (exterior courtyard) substitutes for an expected mass, or a protrusion in the new building borrows a similar protruding element from the Shaughnessy House to reestablish a sense of wholeness. This is particularly true along boulevard René-Lévesque, where the complex pattern of new and old volumes, solid and void, fancy and plain are experienced as both a rhythmic extension of the real streetscape along the north edge of the boulevard *and* as a memory of the types of dwellings which once lined the street.

The tripartite division which recurs throughout the CCA is especially clear when a transverse building section is examined (see page 85). There are two levels of collections storage and laboratory space below grade; at grade there is the curatorial and "systems control" level; and above these are the larger-scaled public spaces of the main floor. (The floor level of the primary rooms of the Shaughnessy House determined the new main floor level, and a heavy stone base, aligned with that of the mansion, was established for the new building.) The section of the new building also reveals the a-b-a relationship of the structural bays, interior space, and programmatic allocation wherein the outer, narrower bays "service" the primary central spaces.

The axial organization of the interior comes alive through the manipulation of light. The combination of vertical top lighting (through skylights) and horizontal side lighting (through windows) deserves attention because the approach to natural light seems, at first, to be entirely familiar. That is, there is apparently nothing new about the white window frames with their small panes of glass, and the top lighting of galleries is quite traditional. However, careful analysis reveals that the windows and skylights (with their integral shading devices) are both rationally placed and sized and designed to bathe the interior in ways which invite movement through the spaces; a play of changing light is provided throughout the day.

fig. 53 Phyllis Lambert, director of the CCA, and Peter Rose, architect, examine a skylight for the new CCA building at the factory. Photograph: Alain Laforest, CCA, 1986.

The primary top lighting sequence commences at the main stair where the Entrance Court is flooded with light from above, emphasizing the verticality of the space and drawing one up the stair to a low rotunda where light comes through a central oculus. This point of light (combined with the window view to the Visitors' Court and a fragment of the Shaughnessy House) arrests movement and sets up a choice of turning right or left. The pull to the left is the strongest, given the dramatic light marking the Centre Hall at the link point between the Shaughnessy House and the new building. Located on the primary axis of the building and the site, the Centre Hall announces the main galleries to the north and the new entrance to the Shaughnessy House to the south. Further to the east, beyond the Centre Hall, is a symmetrically placed second rotunda, also lighted by an oculus and directing one toward the library entrance. At the Library Court another skylight, matching the one over the Entrance Court, completes the U-shape of primary movement through the public level – a path which is symmetrically placed but asymmetrically experienced and which resolves all the early struggles with entry, circulation, and introduction of the institution. At the end of the U, a huge projecting window overlooks the park, reconnecting one with the city and the mountain.

The other very important top lighting system is in the six main exhibition rooms at the centre of the public level and in the

Octagonal Gallery to the west. Rose devised an ingenious set of "collars" around the tops of some of the galleries to activate and reveal natural light. These collars and the complexity of the upper parts of the rooms recall some of Charles Moore's baroque bouncing of light in tall spaces, and introduce through their layering and punctuation a sense of mystery and surprise.

Another large skylight tops the Special Collections Study Room in the Scholars' Wing to the southeast. This three-storey vertical space is entirely glazed on the top (with provision for light control) and has generous windows in the south wall; the experience is similar to being in an exterior courtyard. The bright study room makes an interesting opposition to the necessarily internalized auditorium, its counterpart to the west.

This family of skylights helps to structure a hierarchy of spatial relationships and makes working indoors during the long Montréal winter pleasurable. The builders of the Shaughnessy House knew the rewards of sunlight and greenery and the sound of rain on glass: in the western house a semicircular conservatory, fitted with exquisite stained glass, was added in 1885. The restored conservatory, one of the few remaining in Montréal, can be seen as a symbol of the CCA's exploration of natural light.

The side, horizontal lighting is also intelligent. The CCA had complex environmental and security requirements resulting from the need to protect the collections of books, photographs, drawings, the archives, and other architectural material. The design of the windows, therefore, had to be extremely practical. But the strongest determining factors for their final appearance were not functional. In the divisions of the glass, Peter Rose recalls the traditional wood windows of Montréal institutional buildings, the frames of which were often painted white (fig. 54). He imagined the CCA in the snow, the white aluminum making romantic connections to the winter landscape of Quebec. Phyllis Lambert also felt strongly that white frames would make the windows read much better against the grey stone. She focused on the fact that white so richly captures shade and shadow and creates its own new colours. As she says, thinking back about discussions on the window frames: "white is expansive, subtle. Complexity and richness occur in the umbral areas and the penumbral fringe."

fig. 54 Maison-mère des Soeurs Grises, Montréal. Victor Bourgeau, architect, 1869–80. Photograph: Phyllis Lambert and Richard Pare, 1973.

The division of the glass – the muntins and mullions – is interesting in that Rose has established a hierarchy by varying the scale and proportions of windows in different parts of the building. The Baile Park façade has two grand windows, one elongated to contain the main entrance (fig. 55). These elegant, projecting windows are on the pair of secondary axes (corresponding to the original cadastral lot lines) which run through the new building and adjacent landscape. Along with the two sets of three windows (plus three small ones above) which mark the library (east) and bookstore (west) on either side of these axes, the Entrance Court and Library Court projecting bays bracket the long, austere centre wall section of the north façade.

The east elevation (see page 83) reveals Rose's distinctions between the windows in the primary mass of the new building and those in the two wings. Generally, the windows in the primary mass have smaller panes of glass with vertical emphasis (more formal and institutional) while in the two subsidiary wings (special collections and auditorium) the windows have larger, square panes

of glass (more informal and domestic). This attempt to differentiate a sense of front and back and to proportion the glazing in the wings in relation to the Shaughnessy House windows is not immediately noticed but is absorbed, slowly, as part of the experience of the entire cca composition.

Even more subtle is the adjustment made for the ground floor windows in the primary piece (fig. 56). To express the weight of the building mass above and to respond to the deeply cut horizontal joints in the rusticated stonework below the *piano nobile,* the ground floor windows, most of which are in curatorial offices, have a strong horizontal emphasis, the muntins here corresponding to the joints in the stone coursing. At this point, Rose embedded dwarf aluminum columns in the centre of the window openings to further articulate the lower, weight-bearing portion of the façade. One must, finally, note the intentionally over-scaled lintels of the ground floor windows. These lintels have a pop scale and flare out at the ends in a humorous way. Actually made of two stones which are partially supported by the dwarf aluminum columns, Rose's lintels invite one to recall the best visual games of the mannerists. The closer one looks, the less ordinary the windows seem.

The way light interacts with the building's exterior – particularly the stone – is remarkable, achieving architectural poetry. From summer to winter, morning to night, one façade to another, the changes unfold as an unending dance of shade, shadow and texture (fig. 57). In the detailing, Rose constrasts large-scaled rounded pieces of stone (for example; the bullnose) with tiny shifts in the vertical plane to enjoin a display of Montréal light: the long horizontal shadows cast by the low winter sun; the pinkish glow of a summer morning. The slight battering of the wall (which was a favoured device of both Lutyens and Wagner) reveals very thin ledges of stone that capture light and also make explicit the bearing, the weight of the stone – the constructional relationship to gravity and nature. And through collaboration with lighting designer George Sexton, the performance continues at night: the walls are elegantly uplighted, creating an architectural stage-set for the gardens and the neighbourhood.

If the thoughtful use of stone and artful use of light expressively combine to make the Canadian Centre for Architecture a convincingly northern and Montréal building, then a third ingredient,

fig. 55 Study model for the west half of the north elevation. Office of Peter Rose Architect, 1986.

the metalwork (some elements of which, such as the cornice, have already been mentioned), must not be overlooked. The classical language of the building is simultaneously reinforced and destabilized by the inventive use of aluminum pieces and parts (fig. 58). Maintaining their production-line sharpness and resplendent quality, they are blatantly contemporary. The projecting cornice differentiates the primary volume, the east and west wings and the Shaughnessy House, from, in Rose's words, "the three de-ornamented linkage zones." As stand-in "genera," the cornice, the dwarf columns, the handrails, the fence, the lighting fixtures, and the "stud" inserts in the stone mark out – in related rhythms – the controlled, often sombre spaces and forms of the institution. They are like magical commas and periods which take us through the classical sentences to build the paragraphs of the CCA story. But they are also like quotation marks and, better yet, exclamation marks which activate and surprise. The pieces of toughly detailed aluminum bounce light and enliven surfaces in a welcome attack on the authority of the stone. The jutting cornice on the new building jumps visually to the Shaughnessy House, with its exuberant roofscape of iron cresting and finials, strange chimneys and decorative bands. Images of Quebec metal roofs, spiralling iron stairs, and ornate weathervanes piercing dark moody skies are recalled just before our thoughts return to the high art of Otto Wagner's Vienna Post Office Savings Bank or to the vernacular routine of aluminum television antennae.

This is architecture being critical – questioning, testing, commenting on itself. The architectural language of the CCA takes us

fig. 56 Study model for one typical bay in the north elevation. Office of Peter Rose Architect, 1986.

fig. 57 String course, Scholars' Wing. Photograph: Michel Boulet, CCA, 1988.

beyond the constraints and dictates normally associated with classicism; critical classicism emerges. Again, Tzonis and Lefaivre provide access to these ideas. They promote two partial applications of the classical canon in contemporary practice: syncretism and metastatement, which they say:

can be pessimistic or ironic, polemical or adversarial, but always critical. In the case of syncretism more than one canon is used simultaneously in the same design, even if these are at odds and produce non sequitur effects. In the second case, that of metastatement, a world of higher visual statements is built that refers to the classical canon. Classical segments are used as means of saying something about classicism, they become, in other words, statements within a higher-level metastatement.[5]

In the Canadian Centre for Architecture, classical segments provoke. We are made conscious of the general order, of the unifying iconographic programme, while simultaneously being invited to consider the analogies, the dualities, the oppositions of the parts. If not visually active in the aggressive modern sense, the Canadian Centre for Architecture is exceedingly active in its capacity to intellectually engage us in its multiple and partial canons: antiquity, Wagner, Mies, and greystone Montréal are reclassified in an abstract and uniquely Rose metastatement – *about* and *inside* the classical tradition but also offering surprising escapes from it. The CCA's syncretism results predominantly from a knowledge and institutional representation of architectural history; but understood as a metastatement, the building is intensely conscious of those histories and displays its own material search for new, contemporary "truths"; in this way it is critical of itself. It is, finally, the complex relationship between what the institution is (an architectural museum and study centre), its expression of the classical tradition, and its materially manifested search for alternatives to this tradition that generates the dynamic architecture of the CCA.

* * *

A large proportion of the interior space of the CCA is underground. The organization of the two vault levels in the new building is rational. Long corridors (each more than one hundred metres) run straightforwardly from end to end of the primary rectangular block, under the more elaborate corridors of the curatorial and main floors above. The storage spaces, laboratories, and service spaces are all accessible from these simple yet striking corridors. The walls are white, the floors covered with diagonally placed, black-and-white vinyl tile; and along one side there are continuous fluorescent fixtures, designed by the architects to include the hard-edged aluminum pieces and parts discussed earlier (see page 114). Other than a few doors and some decorative colour breaks in the floor material, there is not much to see except the very long checkerboard floor and the carefully organized pieces of security and safety hardware along the way. The first impression is of a clinical environment; this could be a corridor in a modern hospital. But experience here is consciously layered. A second look generates flashbacks to stately Quebec institutional buildings from the eighteenth and nineteenth centuries. Memories of the geometric, marble-tiled floors of the Grand Séminaire in Quebec City come back as history meets 1988 efficiency.

fig. 58 The Scholars' Wing.
Photograph: Gabor Szilasi, 1988.

Finally one opens the door of a vault to discover row after row of shelving, sometimes installed on rails to allow compaction of the units (see page 115). Few members of the public will see the architectural treasures as they exist here, protected in their basement rooms and constantly monitored by computerized climate-control systems. Selected documents will become part of exhibitions on the floors above and be studied by scholars from throughout the world. Resting on their vanilla-coloured steel shelves, quietly and peacefully hidden from the expressway traffic speeding through tunnels only a few metres beyond their securing walls, one imagines the treasures to be telling stories. And I imagine that these stories are about a new future outside the walls – a place of restored architectural consciousness and community.

In 1987–88, as part of the research for this essay, I was fortunate to have numerous meetings with Phyllis Lambert, director of the CCA, and with Peter Rose, the architect, to discuss the building project. I would like to express my appreciation for their permission to quote them.

1 Walter Benjamin, "Parco centrale," in *Angelus Novus,* by R. Solmi (Turin: Einaudi, 1962), 135.
2 Portia Leggatt, Peter Rose, and Robert Lemire, "Montréal: Ten Buildings to See," *Trace* 1 (April-May-June 1981): 16–29
3 George Baird, introduction, "Montréal: Ten Buildings to See," 17.
4 Alexander Tzonis and Liane Lefaivre, *Classical Architecture: The Poetics of Order* (Cambridge, Mass., and London: MIT Press, 1986), 6.
5 Tzonis and Lefaivre, *Classical Architecture,* 280.

The CCA Site:
An Illustrated Chronology,
1694–1988

ROBERT LEMIRE

The seven maps in this section show the urban development of the area surrounding the CCA building and gardens. The area depicted is the Dorchester Plateau, delimited by the sharp rise of Mount Royal to the north and the steep decline at the edge of the escarpment to the south. Above boulevard René-Lévesque the land was part of the original Sulpician Domain. It holds, with the Séminaire de Saint-Sulpice in old Montréal, the oldest built evidence of settlement on the island of Montréal. The maps include the present sites and buildings of the great founding institutions of Montréal which surround the CCA building and gardens: the Maison-mère des Sœurs Grises to the east, the Sulpician Domain to the north, the Maison-mère de la Congrégation de Notre-Dame (now Dawson College) to the west.

The historical maps were constructed from a number of sources, but always starting from the current offical city map, and peeling backward. The dates were chosen to show significant change in the urban fabric and land use; their titles reflect the nature of the changes. The maps are based on the following sources: Plant de la mission de la Montagne, artist unknown (Archives nationales de France, 1694 [see page 141]); Alan Stewart, Daniel Thibault, "Farm concessions on the island of Montréal, 1663" (adapted from Marcel Trudel, *Montréal, la formation d'une société 1642–1663* [Montréal: Fides, 1976]); James Cane, *Topographical and Pictorial Map of the City of Montreal* (Montreal: Robert W.S. Mackay, 1846); Henry W. Hopkins, *Atlas of the City and Island of Montreal* (n.p.: Provincial Survey and Publishing Co., 1879); Charles Edward Goad, *Atlas of the City of Montreal and Vicinity in Four Volumes* (Montreal: Chas. E. Goad, 1912–14); Ville de Montreal,

Service de l'habitation et de l'urbanisme, utilisation du sol, plans nos. 226–25, 26, 27; 227–25, 26, 27; Ville de Montreal, Service de l'habitation et du développement urbain, utilisation du sol, plans nos. 226–25, 26, 27; 227–25, 26, 27; P25, Séminaire de Saint-Sulpice, bobine 285, concession 627, Service des Archives, Université de Montréal; minute notarié, 23 juillet 1690, Antoine Adhémar, Archives Nationales du Québec, Montréal; carte 11-1702, Archives de la Ville de Montréal; bobine 797, concessions 627 à 636, Archives Nationales du Québec, Montréal. The cartography is by Daniel Thibeault; assistance was provided by Alan Stewart and Brian Young. (The maps for 1850 and 1879 do not show the built area west of the city boundary because no maps exist for this period.)

*   Future site of Shaughnessy House

———--—— City limits

1694 Fort

1659 Concessions granted south of Sulpician Domain (1)

1675 Indian Mission established (2)

ca. 1680 Wooden fort built (3)

ca. 1685 Fort de la montagne built of stone on site of wooden fort by François Vachon de Belmont, superior of Saint-Sulpice (3)

1694 Indian village destroyed by fire (2)

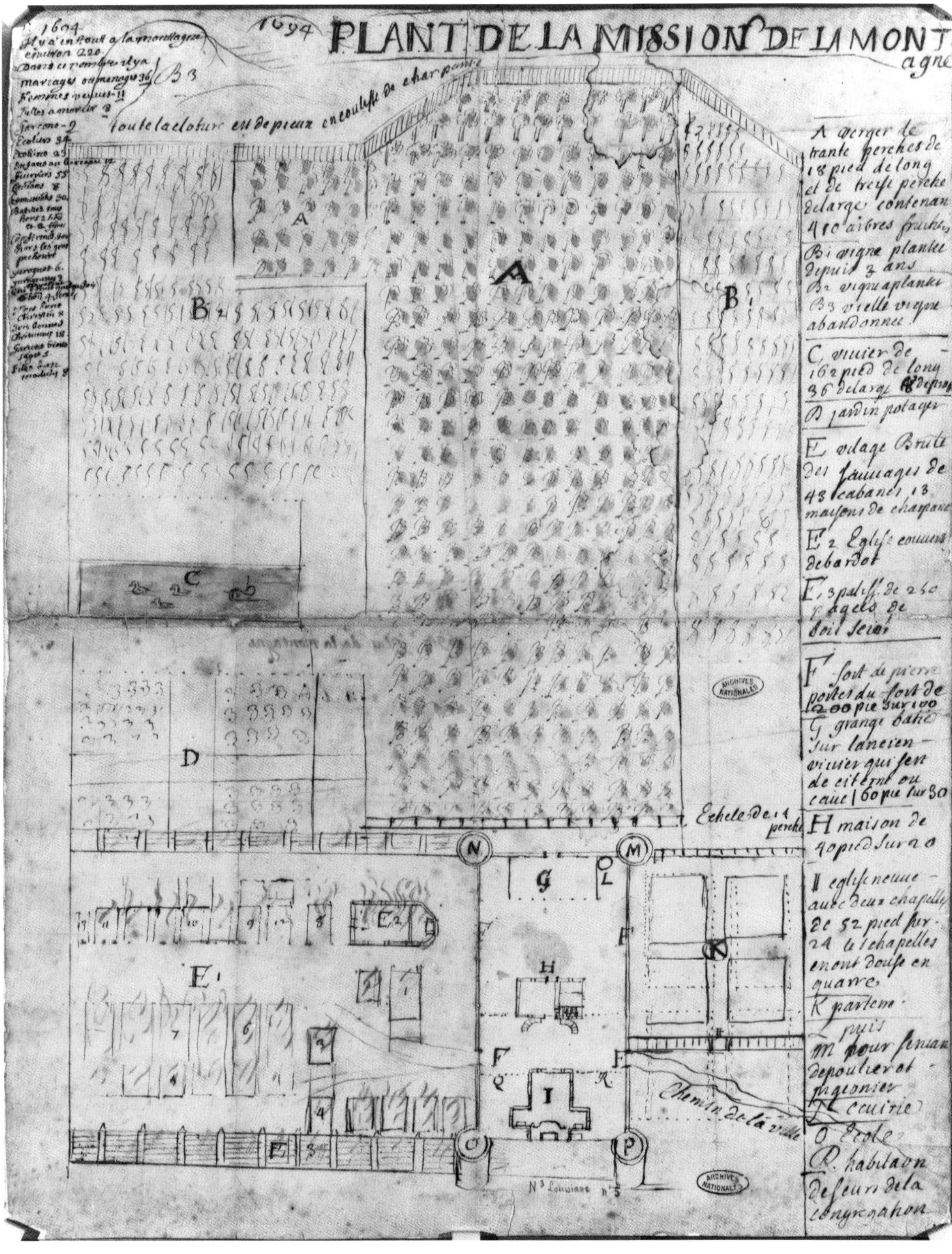

fig. 59 Plant de la mission de la montagne, 1694. Archives nationales, Paris, cartes et plans (NIII Canada 12).

1850 Farms and Villas

Fort de la montagne (1)

ca. 1700 Grand chemin de la haute folie (Dorchester Street) opened along the south boundary of the Sulpician Domain (2)

ca. 1700 Long pond built west of Fort de la montagne (3)

ca. 1770 Orchards planted on edge of escarpment south of Sulpician Domain (4)

1801 Long pond extended (3)

1803 "Château Saint-Antoine" built for William McGillivray (5)

ca. 1835 House built for Louis Guy (7)

ca. 1835 House built for Georges Desbarats (6)

ca. 1840 "Hillside" built for Thomas S. Judah (9)

1840 "Le Bocage" built for Jean-Roch Rolland (8)

ca. 1845 "Hutton Villa" built for John H. Maitland (11)

1845 Canada Baptist College (10)

1847 Rue Sherbrooke extended westward through Sulpician Domain (12)

1850 "Mon Bonheur II" built for William Masson (13)

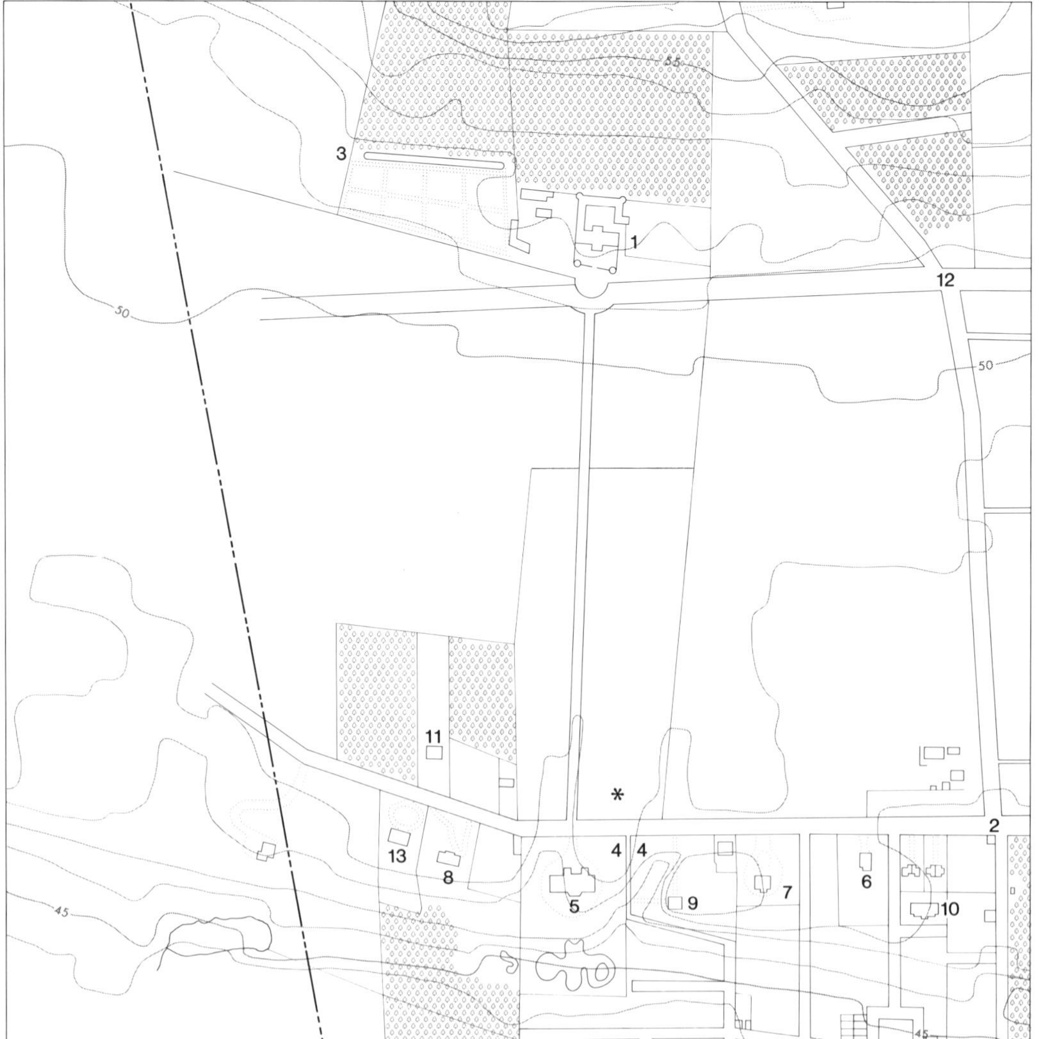

fig. 60 Château des messieurs de Saint Sulpice, or Fort de la montagne (1). Drawing: Charles Dawson Shanley, 1847. McCord Museum of Canadian History, Montréal.

fig. 61 "Mon Bonheur," Wilfred Masson's house (13). Photograph: Richard Pare and Phyllis Lambert, 1973.

1879 Urbanization

Southern towers of Fort de la montagne
(1)

1854 Demolition of northern section of Fort de la montagne
Construction of Grand Seminaire begins (2)

1857 Construction of Grand Seminaire completed (2)

1862 Rue Sainte-Catherine extended through Sulpician Domain (3)

1868 Rue Saint-Marc opened (4)

1868–88 Maison-mère des Sœurs Grises built (5)

1870–72 Collège de Montréal built adjoining Grand Séminaire to the east (6)

1871–72 Rue du Fort opened (7)

1873 "Château Sainte-Antoine" demolished, except entrance gates, for subdivision (8)

1874–75 Duncan McIntyre / Robert Brown houses (Shaughnessy House) built (9)

fig. 62 Grand séminaire de Montréal (2). Photograph: Richard Pare and Phyllis Lambert, 1973.

fig. 64 The entrance gates of Chateau Sainte-Antoine (8). Photograph: William Notman and Son, 1899. McCord Museum of Canadian History, Notman Photographic Archives (130, 260-II).

fig. 63 Maison-mère des Soeurs-Grises (5). Photograph: Richard Pare and Phyllis Lambert, 1973.

fig. 65 The Shaughnessy House (9). Photograph: Brian Merrett, 1973. CCA (PH1987:1098).

1912 Metropolis

1886 Strathcona House built (1)

1889 Canadian Pacific Railway opened (2)

1892–93 Maison Saint-Joseph, home for the elderly, built by the Little Sisters of the Poor (3)

1893 Franciscan monastery established in former Jean-Roch Rolland house and chapel built (4)

1905–08 Maison-mère de la Congrégation de Notre-Dame built (5)

fig. 66 Strathcona House (1). Photograph: William Notman and Son, ca. 1907.
McCord Museum of Canadian History, Notman Photographic Archives (4267 view).

fig. 68 Franciscan chapel (4). Photograph: Gabor Szilasi, 1988.

fig. 69 Maison-mère de la Congrégation de Notre-Dame (5). Photograph: Gabor
Szilasi, 1988.

fig. 67 Maison Saint-Joseph (3). Photograph: Gabor Szilasi, 1988.

1974 Destruction

1939–41 Shaughnessy House purchased by the
Sisters of Service and converted into a
rooming house for working women (1)

1941 Strathcona House demolished (2)

1969 Houses demolished to widen Dorchester
Street into boulevard (3)

1972 Trans-Canada Highway opened (4)

fig. 70 Aerial view, looking east, showing demolition for the Atwater and Guy access to the autoroute Ville Marie. (3). Photograph: Paul Henri Talbot, *La Presse,* 1970.

1988 Reconstruction

1974 Shaughnessy House officially designated
an historic site by Environment Canada,
and a *monument historique* by the ministère
des Affaires culturelles du Quebec (1)

1975–88 Office building, hotels and
condominiums built along boulevard
Dorchester (2)

1985–88 Centre Canadien d'Architecture /
Canadian Centre for Architecture built,
and Shaughnessy House restored as part
of it (3)

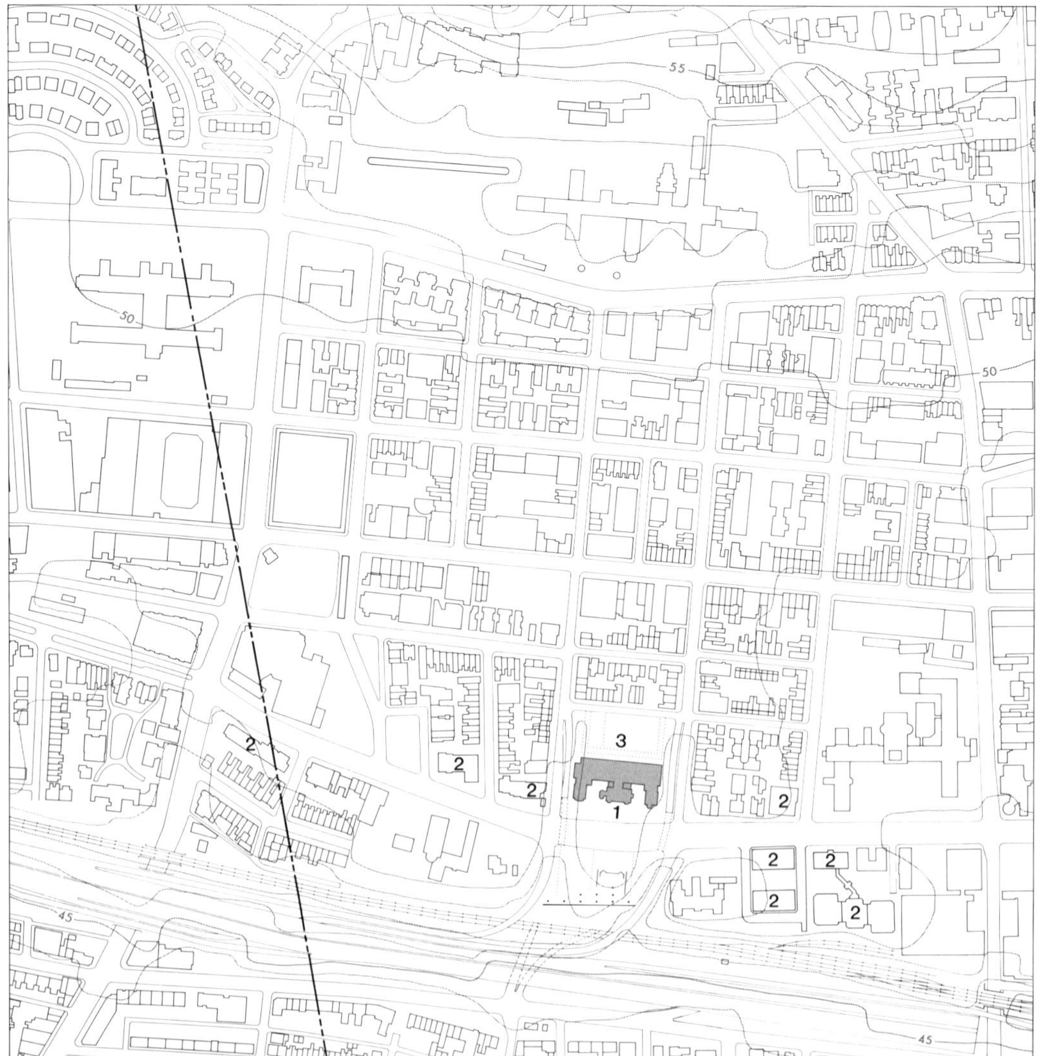

fig. 71 View from the southwest of the CCA Garden under construction, and the Canadian Centre for Architecture (3). Photograph: Geoffrey James, December 1988.

Building and Gardens:
Participants, Chronology,
and Specifications

HELEN MALKIN

Client: Centre Canadien d'Architecture /
Canadian Centre for Architecture,
Phyllis Lambert, Director

Project team
Client's representative for the construction project: Guy Doré
Head of collection services: Lori Gross
Head librarian: Daphne Roloff
Curator of prints and drawings: Mimi Cazort
Curator of the photographs collection: Richard Pare
Head archivist: Robert Desaulniers
Manager of conservation and preservation: Siegfried Rempel
Coordinator of installations: Robert Anderson

Architect: Peter Rose Architect

Architect: Peter Rose
Design team: Peter Rose, Erik Marosi, Nicholas Garrison
Project architect, new building: William Steinberg
Project architect, Shaughnessy House: Karl Pinault
Project team: André Avel, Paul Chiasson, Manuel Gimenez, Hélène
Sophie Lemieux, Luciana Mastropasqua, Marie-Paule Macdonald,
Mark Poddubiuk, Deborah Rosen, Susan Ross, Leigh Barnett-Shapiro,
Martin Troy, Leah van der Voort
Special renderings: Jill Alexander, Gregory Henriquez, David Kepron

Consulting architect: Phyllis Lambert Architecte

Associate architect: Erol Argun Architecte

Architect: Erol Argun
Assistant architects: Juho Kim, Liliane Latinovic
Construction supervisors: Russ Coffin, Zeinab El Kachab
Specifications: Robert Richard

Architect of the CCA Garden: Melvin Charney

Architect: Melvin Charney
Design team: Natalie Jean, Francine Péloquin, Martin St. Denis,
Martin Vincent

Restoration architect: Bilodeau St-Louis Architectes

Architect: Denis St-Louis
Assistant architects: Bernard S. Gagné, Patrice B. Lapointe,
Chantal Perreault
Assistant technicians for design and supervision: Jacques Coquereau,
Christine Côté, Michel Côté, Marc Olivier Drouin, Roger Landry,
Jocelyn Martel, Marc Pouliot, Marcel St-Louis.

Consultants

Structural engineer: Nicolet Chartrand Knoll Ltd.

Mechanical / electrical engineer: The ECE Group Ltd.

Soil testing: Inspec-Sol Inc.

Soil engineer: Lupien, Rosenberg et Associés Inc.

Landscape architect: Gerrard and Mackars Landscape Architects

Lighting: George Sexton Associates

Security: Joseph M. Chapman, Inc.

Audio / visual: Boyce Nemec Designs

Acoustics: Lewis S. Goodfriend & Associates

Special glazing: James Carpenter Design

Signage and graphics: François Dallegret

Contractors

New building: Divco Ltd.

New Building, public level interior:
P & R Desjardins Construction Inc.

Shaughnessy House: Les Constructions J. & R. Duhamel Ltée

Landscape: Aldershot Landscape Contractors Ltd.

Restoration Artisans

Interior woodwork:
Doors, mouldings, window frames: Camille Mouillot Inc.
Tea room, entry halls, stairs: Martin Proulx Inc.

Exterior woodwork: Sculpture Fonctionnelle de Montréal Inc.

Conservatory glass and metal restoration:
Les Solariums Solagro Enrg.

Engraved and coloured glass: Studio du Verre

Plasterwork: Revêtement 2000 Québec Inc.

BUILDING CHRONOLOGY

17 November 1973 — Historic Sites and Monuments Board of Canada, Environment Canada, recommends designation of Shaughnessy House as an historic site.

6 February 1974 — Ministère des Affaires culturelles du Québec designates the Shaughnessy House an historic monument.

11 February 1974 — Phyllis Lambert submits a formal offer to purchase the Shaughnessy House from the Sisters of Service of Canada

14 February 1974 — Minister of the Environment, Canada, designates the Shaughnessy House an historic site.

16 April 1974 — Phyllis Lambert purchases the Shaughnessy House from the Sisters of Service of Canada.

6 September 1979 — The Centre Canadien d'Architecture / Canadian Centre for Architecture is incorporated in accordance with part 2 of the Canada Corporations Act (for non-profit corporations).

31 March 1981 — "Maison Shaughnessy Montréal, Québec. Rapport d'Entretien Architecture Mécanique et Structure" on the Shaughnessy House submitted by Bilodeau St-Louis to Heritage Montréal.

May 1981 — Les Constructions J. & R. Duhamel Ltée, under the supervision of Bilodeau St-Louis Architectes, begins preventative maintenance of the Shaughnessy House

October 1983 — Peter Rose begins design of the CCA

13 January 1984 — Canadian Museums Association officially recognizes the CCA as a museum.

1 March 1984 — Department of Communications, Canada, designates the CCA a "Class A Institution" for the purposes of the Cultural Property Export and Import Act.

13 June 1984 — CCA purchases the Shaughnessy House from Phyllis Lambert.

20 June 1984 — Montréal City Council adopts resolution in which all land on the block north of boulevard René-Lévesque which is not part of the Shaughnessy House property be donated to the CCA with the understanding that the CCA create and maintain it as a green space.

18 March 1985 — Les Constructions J.& R. Duhamel Ltée begins work on phase 1 of the Shaughnessy House (removal of all non-original partitions and additions).

25 April 1985 — Les Constructions J.& R. Duhamel Ltée begins work on phase 2 of the Shaughnessy House (restoration of east and north-east walls).

29 April 1985 — Contract between CCA and Peter Rose Architect for the "Renovation of the Shaughnessy House and construction of the Canadian Centre for Architecture and design plans and supervision of the surrounding area."

Contract between Peter Rose Architect and Erol Argun Architecte.

Contract between Peter Rose Architect and Bilodeau St-Louis Architectes for restoration of the Shaughnessy House.

Contracts between Peter Rose Architect and Nicolet Chartrand Knoll Ltd.; The ECE Group Ltd.; George Sexton Associates; Joseph M. Chapman Inc.; Gerrard and Mackars Landscape Architects; Boyce Nemec Designs.

13 May 1985 — Ceremony initiating the construction of the new building of the CCA.

18 June 1985 — Agreement between CCA and Divco Ltd. for phase 1 work (excavation and foundations to grade).

19 December 1985	Agreement between CCA and Divco Ltd., for phase 2 work (construction and enclosure of building above grade, and installation of primary electrical and mechanical systems).
16 October 1986	Montréal City Council adopts a resolution granting an emphyteutic lease of 75 years for the land south of boulevard René-Lévesque (the CCA Garden) to the CCA.
4 December 1986	Les Constructions J.& R. Duhamel Ltée begins phase 3 work on Shaughnessy House (interior and exterior restoration).
15 January 1987	Agreement between CCA and Divco Ltd. for phase 3 work (interior finishes of vault and curatorial levels).
8 April 1987	Ministère des Affaires culturelles du Québec announces competition for a sculpture for the CCA Garden as part of its programme "Intégrations des arts à l'architecture et à l'environnement."
5 May 1987	Contract between CCA and Aldershot Landscape Contractors Ltd. for landscaping of Baile Park.
7 August 1987	Ministère des Affaires culturelles du Québec convenes jury for CCA sculpture competition.
16 September 1987	CCA announces Melvin Charney as winner of CCA sculpture competition and designer of CCA Garden.
25 January 1988	Contract between CCA and P & R Desjardins Construction Inc. for phase 4 work (new building public level interior).
8 June 1988	Aldershot Landscape Contractors Ltd. begins work on the CCA Garden.
7 May 1989	Official opening of the CCA.

AREAS (square metres)

Site

Block north of boulevard René-Lévesque

New building (foot print)	3,036	
Shaughnessy House (foot print)	508	
Baile Park, courtyards, and lawns	7,136	
Roadways	1,798	
Total	12,478	(1.2 hectares / 3 acres)

Block south of boulevard René-Lévesque

CCA Garden	8,388	(.8 hectares / 2 acres)
Grand total	20,866	(2.0 hectares / 5 acres)

Floor Areas

New building

Vault, level 1	2,880	
Vault, level 2	2,880	
Curatorial, level 3	2,880	
Public, level 4	2,880	
Mezzanine, level 5	612	
Total	12,132	(130,600 sq ft)

Shaughnessy House

Service, level 3	510	
Public, level 4	492	
Director's office, level 5	418	
Administrative, level 6	380	
Total	1,800	(19,400 sq ft)
Grand total:	13,932	(150,000 sq ft)

EXTERIOR BUILDING HEIGHTS

New building (at Baile Park):

Height of building from bottom slab to grade	7.87m	(25ft. 10in.)
Height of building from grade to parapet	11.17m	(36ft. 7in.)

Shaughnessy House (at boulevard René-Lévesque)

Height of building from bottom slab to grade	1.67m	(5ft. 5in.)
Height of building from grade to parapet	13.48m	(44ft. 3in.)

BUILDING COMPONENTS

New building

Structure

In-situ reinforced concrete frame and flat slab structure; steel roof trusses at auditorium; column bays of main block: in east–west direction, all bays 6.3m; in north–south direction, 6.3m, 9.4m, 6.3m (public level), 6.3m, 4.7m, 4.7m, 6.3m (all other levels).

Exterior Wall section (public level, at galleries)

Masonry cavity walls consisting of 16.5cm limestone, 2.54cm cavity, 20.3cm concrete block, 2.54cm cavity, 5.0cm rigid insulation, 1.3cm water resistant gypsum board, fiberglass wool insulation between 15.2cm metal studs, 6 ml vapour barrier, 25.7cm cavity to clear columns, 15.2cm metal studs, 1.9cm plywood, 1.6cm gypsum board.

Roof sections

30.5cm concrete slab, primer, 2 ply 6 ml vapour barrier, double layer of 5.5cm insulation, flexible waterproof membrane with elastomer modified bitumen (all roofs except auditorium); steel decking, 1.9cm plywood, 6ml vapour barrier, 10cm insulation, 1.9cm plywood, 16oz lead-coated copper (auditorium); all counter flashings covered in 16oz lead-coated copper.

Exterior Finishes

Walls
16.5cm to 13.9cm self-supporting bush hammered Trenton Limestone (rusticated base and ashlar main body); 11.4cm pinned bush hammered Trenton limestone (entablature).

Windows
White Duranar XL finished aluminum frames, double-glazed Solex low emissivity glass with laminated clear Saflex Interlayer ultraviolet filter.

Skylights
Clear anodized aluminum frames, double-glazed Solex low emissivity glass with laminated translucent white Saflex Interlayer ultraviolet filter (gallery skylights); clear anodized aluminum frames, double-glazed PPG Solarban Monovision glass with laminated clear Saflex Interlayer ultraviolet filter (other skylights).

Ornamental metal
(All metal is clear anodized aluminum unless otherwise noted.) Assembly of extruded sections, perforated plates and sand cast brackets (cornice); assembly of plates and extruded sections (dwarf columns, protective canopies); sheets and flat bars fastened to metal sub-structure (entrance vestibule); assembly of extruded sections and perforated plates with stainless steel handrails and connecting plates (balustrade); checkered plates mounted on metal doors (service entrances).

Interior Finishes

(All finishes are chemically stable to prevent the release of vapours or gases.)

Floors
Public level: 1.9cm honed Peribonka black granite laid on 5.7cm concrete and sand bed (Entrance Court, Hall); 1.9cm honed Peribonka black granite steps with polished Peribonka black granite risers (Entrance Court stairs); Pacific Strong waterborne acrylic / polyurethane finished 1.9cm Canadian maple strip flooring on double layer of 1.3cm plywood on neoprene resilient cushions (galleries); wool carpet (library, Scholars' Wing, auditorium).
Curatorial level: vinyl tile (corridors); nylon carpet (offices, work areas).
Vault levels: vinyl tile (corridors, laboratories); Ceilcote water based acrylic paint on concrete (vaults).

Unglazed black ceramic tile (washrooms on all levels).

Walls
(Unless otherwise noted all wall assemblies mounted on steel studs; accoustical insulation inserted as required.)
Public level: 5cm Trenton limestone revetment (Entrance Court, ground level); 5cm Trenton limestone revetment fastened to concrete slab or columns (column at entrance to galleries, fascia at library reading room, columns and fascia at Scholars's Wing); 1.9cm clear lacquered Canadian maple panels mounted to 1.9cm plywood on 1.3cm gypsum board (Entrance Court, Rotundas, Library Court, Scholars' Wing

fascia); 1.9cm clear lacquered Canadian maple panels mounted to 1.9cm plywood on 15.2cm wood studs (auditorium); 1.6cm gypsum board on 1.9cm plywood (galleries, hall); double layer 1.3cm gypsum board (all other areas).
Curatorial level: double layer of 1.3cm gypsum board (all areas).
Vault levels: double and triple layer of 1.3cm and 1.6cm gypsum board (corridors, vaults); 8.2cm stainless steel sheet insulated panels (cool and cold photographs storage vaults).

Glazed white ceramic tiles; polished Peribonka black granite toilet partitions with maple doors (washrooms on all levels); painted wood baseboards (all levels).

Ceilings
Public level: two layers of 1.0cm gypsum board or acoustical insulation covered with flame retardant fabric stretched between clear anodized aluminum ribs, attached to metal suspension system (auditorium); single or double layer of 1.3cm gypsum board on metal framing (Rotundas, galleries); double layer of 1.3cm gypsum board attached to metal suspension system (all other areas).
Curatorial level: double layer of 1.3cm gypsum board attached to metal suspension system (corridors, offices); 61cm x 61cm Donn Ceiling System perforated acoustical metal pan attached to metal suspension system (work areas).
Vault levels: 61cm x 61cm Donn Ceiling System perforated acoustical metal pan attached to metal suspension system (corridors, laboratories); painted concrete (vaults).

Casework and built in furniture
Public level: modified Glasbau Hahn wall vitrine (hall display cases); all casework is either clear lacquered Canadian maple or white lacquered wood; writing surfaces are grey or black lineoleum.
Curatorial level: all casework is either clear lacquered Canadian maple or white lacquered wood; writing surfaces are white arborite.
Vault levels: work surfaces are either clear lacquered Canadian maple, resin impregnated Scioto sandstone or stainless steel (laboratories).

Ornamental metal
(All metal is clear anodized aluminum unless otherwise noted.) Assembly of extruded sections and perforated plates with stainless steel hand rails and stainless steel connecting plates (balustrade); assembly of extruded sections (custom lighting fixtures, pendant for track lights in galleries); rigidtex and smooth stainless steel sheets (elevator cabs); perforated clear anodized aluminum plates on metal substructure (projection booth).

Doors
(all levels) Clear or double-glazed laminated patterned glass panelled doors with clear lacquered or painted Canadian maple frames; clear lacquered Canadian maple or painted solid doors; steel fire doors.

Windows
Clear lacquered Canadian maple frames with double-glazed laminated patterned glass (curatorial and scholars' offices); clear lacquered or painted Canadian maple frames with clear glass (all other areas).

Shaughnessy House Restoration

Exterior

Roof finishes
New slate shingles to match original shingles on mansard; restoration of cast-iron cresting.

Stonework
Refacing or reconstruction with new Trenton limestone as needed.

Windows
Reconstruction of wood, windows modified to accommodate double glazing; new windows inserted in northern central section of level 5, and new skylights inserted on level 6.

Doors
Restoration of original wood doors.

Cornice and dormers
Reconstruction of wood and galvanized sheet steel ornament.

Interior

Service, level 3: contemporary construction of floors (nylon carpet), walls, and ceilings (suspended gypsum board); partial reconstruction of wood window surrounds and baseboards.
Public, level 4: restoration and reconstruction of plaster walls, ceilings, cornice and medallions; restoration of wood stairs, railings, doors, Tearoom floor, entrance hall floors, wall panelling, baseboards, window surrounds and shutters; restoration and replication of engraved glass and marble floor in conservatory; wool carpet in reception and conference rooms.
Office of the Director, level 5: contemporary construction of floors (wool carpet), walls, and ceilings (suspended gypsum board); reconstruction of cornice plasterwork and wood baseboards; restoration of wood doors.
Administrative, level 6: contemporary construction of floors (nylon carpet), walls, ceilings (suspended gypsum board), doors, and baseboards.

OPERATING CHARACTERISTICS

Mechanical

Automated centrally controlled system of steam and chilled water regulates electronically cleaned filtered air. The following temperatures and levels of humidity are maintained:

Area	Temperature,°C (variance ± 1.5 °C)	Relative humidity, % (variance $\pm 2\%$)	
		Summer	Winter
Galleries	22	50	30
Public areas	22	50	30
Office areas	22	50	30
Collection vaults	20	43	43
Photographs vault (cool storage)	12.5	40	40
Photographs vault (cold storage)	4.5	40	40

The vault mechanical system reacts more quickly than other areas of the building to correct temperature and humidity variances.

Fire protection

Halon gas system (collection storage and collection work areas); hydraulic dry pipe sprinkler system (all other areas).

Lighting

Public level: motorized adjustable louver system located between the skylight and the gallery ceilings regulates ambient daylight directed into lantern and on vaulted ceiling surfaces; exposed or recessed track mounted incandescent fixtures (galleries); surface mounted, track mounted and recessed incandescant fixtures (auditorium); surface mounted, track mounted or recessed incandescent fixtures (all other spaces).
Curatorial level: ultraviolet filtered fluorescent parabolic fixtures; surface mounted incandescent fixtures; incandescent or ultraviolet filtered fluorescent task lighting.
Vault levels: ultraviolet filtered fluorescent fixtures on grid suspension system.

Communications Grid

Power, telephone and computer data-base lines in underfloor raceway grid system on curatorial and public levels, with outlets located in the library, galleries, bookstore, curatorial, and scholars' offices. Wall and slab conduits supply power, telephone and computer data-base lines to vaults.

LANDSCAPE

Baile Park, Courtyards and Lawns

Planting

Trees
Ulmus Americana / American elm (bordering rue Baile); *Fraxinus pensylvanica 'Marshall's Seedless'* / Marshall's seedless green ash (bordering expressway ramps); *Acer saccharum* / sugar maple (bordering interior roadway perpendicular to building); *Quercus robur 'Fastigiata'* / Pyramidal English oak (partially bordering interior roadway parallel to building); *Robinia Pseudoacacia* / black locust (Visitors' and Scholars' Courtyards).

Shrubs
Viburnum opulus / European high bush cranberry (bordering fence at northern edge of Baile Park); *Euonymus alatas 'Compactus'* / compact burning bush (bordering retaining wall at southern edge of Baile Park).

Vines
Parthenocissus tricuspidata / Boston ivy (expressway ramp walls); *Vinca minor* / periwinkle (edge of shrub-bed bordering fence at northern edge of Baile Park).

Perennials
Aconitum henryii 'Sparks Variety' / Monkshood; *Anchusa azurea 'Dropmore'* / Italian Bugloss; 5 varieties of *Delphinium* / Delphinium; *Liatris scariosa 'Alba'* / White Gayfeathers; *Lilium* / lilies; *Lythrum salicaria 'Mordem Pink'* / Purple Loosestrife; *Paeonia officinalis rubra plena* / red peony; 3 varieties of *Phlox paniculata* / summer phlox; *Salvia azurea Grandiflora* / Pitcher sage; *Salvia superba* / Superb sage; *Veronica 'Crater Lake Blue'* / Crater Lake Speedwell (edge of shrub bed bordering fence at northern edge of Baile Park).

Bulbs
Crocus purpureus 'Grandiflorus' / Purple crocus (lawn); *Narcissus Unsurpassable* / Unsurpassable daffodil (lawn bordering north façade of building).

Grasses
Touchdown Kentucky bluegrass, Nugget Kentucky bluegrass,
Manhattan Perennial ryegrass, Jamestowns Chewings fescue (lawn).

Paving

Concrete unit pavers (interior roadways); Peribonka granite (entrance
footpath).

Fences, Gateposts and Retaining Walls

8.9 bush hammered Trenton limestone facing and 13.9cm coping on in
situ poured concrete with an assembly of clear anodized aluminum plates
and extruded sections (perimeter fence north of new building); 8.9cm
bush hammered Trenton limestone facing on in situ poured concrete
with stainless steel plate lantern and clear anodized aluminum plates
(gateposts); dry-laid rock-faced Trenton limestone with 13.9cm bush
hammered Trenton limestone copings (retaining walls); dry-laid bush-
hammered Trenton limestone (wall south of Shaughnessy House).

CCA Garden

Planting

Trees
Acer platanoides 'Emerald Queen' / Emerald Queen Norway maple (on
median strip and bordering boulevard René-Lévesque); *Fraxinus
pensylvanica 'Marshall's Seedless* / Marshall's seedless green ash
(bordering western expressway ramp); *Malus species* / northern spy,
Cortland, Close, and Lobo apple trees (orchard); *Acer saccharinum* /
silver maple and *Fagus grandifolia* / beech (bordering interior walkways).

Shrubs
Viburnum opulus / European high bush cranberry (bordering expressway
ramps)

Vines
Parthenocissus tricuspidata / Boston ivy (arcade); *Clematis paniculata* /
sweet autumn clematis (cadastral line walls).

Roses
Rosa rugosa 'Seville' / Seville rose (on escarpment slope); *Rosa rugosa cv.* /
Red Shrub rose (cadastral line walls).

Perennials
Aquilegia hybrida / columbines (orchard and cadastral line walls);
Centaurea cyanus / cornflower, *Oxalis cernua* / buttercup, *Penstemon
fruticosus* / beard tongue (orchard).

Bulbs
Scilla / Scilla (meadow).

Grasses
Touchdown Kentucky bluegrass, Nugget Kentucky bluegrass,
Manhattan Perennial ryegrass, Jamestowns Chewings fescue (orchard,
lawn); *Festuca Rubra* / red fescue (orchard, escarpment).

Paving

Limestone screening.

Cadastral Line Walls

Limestone fieldstone.

Structures

Sandblast finished in situ poured concrete with 13.9cm bush hammered
Trenton limestone copings and pink Laurentian granite string course
(the arcades); 8.9cm bush hammered Trenton limestone facing and
13.9cm coping with pink Laurentian granite base course on in situ
poured concrete (Belvedere wall); sandblast finished in situ poured
concrete, welded stainless steel with mat finish, 24oz copper sheets on
treated wood (allegorical columns).

Notes to the Portfolios

Portfolio 1 (pages 33–54)

Trenton limestone blocks at carrières Saint-Marc,
Saint-Marc des-Carrières, Quebec
Gelatin silver print
23.6 x 33.3cm
September 1987
Laura Volkerding
CCA

The Shaughnessy House at the start of construction
Gelatin silver print
26.4 x 34.5cm
November 1985
David Miller
CCA

The construction site after completion of
second vault floor
Gelatin silver print
26.4 x 34.5cm
September 1985
David Miller
CCA

Auditorium wing of the new building,
and the Shaughnessy house conservatory
Gelatin silver print
26.4 x 34.5cm
January 1987
David Miller
CCA

The partially constructed north elevation,
new building
Gelatin silver print
26.4 x 34.5cm
January 1987
David Miller
CCA

Bay window in the drawing room,
Shaughnessy House
Gelatin silver print
39.7 x 49.9cm
February 1987
Clara Gutsche
CCA

Staircase, Shaughnessy House.
Gelatin silver print
49.9 x 39.7cm
February 1987
Clara Gutsche
CCA

Reception and dining rooms looking toward the
entrance hall, Shaughnessy House
Gelatin silver print
33.8 x 26.5cm
February 1987
Clara Gutsche
CCA

The wood frame for Serlian dormer window,
Shaughnessy House
Gelatin silver print
26.5 x 33.8cm
April 1987
Clara Gutsche
CCA

View through Tearoom to conservatory,
Shaughnessy House
Gelatin silver print
49.9 x 39.7cm
February 1987
Clara Gutsche
CCA

Ductwork adjacent to the octagonal gallery,
new building
Gelatin silver print
49.9 x 39.7cm
June 1987
Clara Gutsche
CCA

Mechanical room on second vault level,
new building
Gelatin silver print
33.8 x 26.5cm
April 1987
Clara Gutsche
CCA

The Scholars' Wing, new building
Gelatin silver print
33.8 x 26.5cm
January 1987
Clara Gutsche
CCA

View of the main galleries from across the
Entrance Court, new building
Gelatin silver print
26.5 x 33.8cm
June 1987
Clara Gutsche
CCA

Mock-up of one of the square galleries,
new building
Gelatin silver print
48.2 x 38.2cm
March 1988
Clara Gutsche
CCA

Partially constructed storage racks in the
photographs collection vault, new building
Gelatin silver print
26.5 x 33.8cm
January 1988
Clara Gutsche
CCA

The prints and drawings collection vault,
new building
Gelatin silver print
26.5 x 33.8cm
August 1987
Clara Gutsche
CCA

The north elevation of the new building,
showing partially completed cornice
Gelatin silver print
26.4 x 34.5cm
September 1988
David Miller
CCA

The Entrance Court, new building
Gelatin silver print
34.5 x 26.4cm
June 1988
David Miller
CCA

View through the Shaughnessy House conservatory
toward the auditorium
Gelatin silver print
34.8 x 49.2cm
September 1987
Laura Volkerding
CCA

Portfolio 2 (pages 79–86)

Site Plan of the CCA, including the CCA Garden
by Melvin Charney
Black ink on matt Strathmore Series 400
paper
182.9 x 86.3cm
1988
Gregory Henriquez, Jill Alexander, and
Marie-Paule Macdonald, delineators
Peter Rose Architect

North Elevation
Black ink on matt Strathmore Series 400
paper
86.3 x 256.5cm
1988
Gregory Henriquez and Jill Alexander,
delineators
Peter Rose Architect

Plan of the Public Level
Black ink on matt Strathmore Series 400
paper
86.3 x 139.7cm
1988
Jill Alexander and Gregory Henriquez,
delineators
Peter Rose Architect

West Elevation
Black ink on matt Strathmore Series 400
paper
86.3 x 139.7cm
1988
Gregory Henriquez and David Kepron,
delineators
Peter Rose Architect

East Elevation
Black ink on matt Strathmore Series 400
paper
86.3 x 139.7cm
1988
Gregory Henriquez and David Kepron,
delineators
Peter Rose Architect

South Elevation
Black ink on matt Strathmore Series 400
paper
86.3 x 256.5cm
1988
Gregory Henriquez and David Kepron,
delineators
Peter Rose Architect

Plan of the Curatorial Level
Black ink on matt Strathmore Series 400
paper
86.3 x 139.7cm
1988
Gregory Henriquez and Jill Alexander,
delineators
Peter Rose Architect

Transverse Section
Black ink on matt Strathmore Series 400
paper
86.3 x 139.7cm
1988
Gregory Henriquez and David Kepron,
delineators
Peter Rose Architect

Longitudinal Section
Black ink on matt Strathmore Series 400
paper
86.3 x 256.5cm
1988
David Kepron and Gregory Henriquez,
delineators
Peter Rose Architect

Exterior Wall Detail
Black ink on matt Strathmore Series 400
paper
86.3 x 182.9cm
1988
Gregory Henriquez and David Kepron,
delineators
Peter Rose Architect

Portfolio 3 (pages 104–19)

*Partial view of the south elevation
at the Shaughnessy House*
Chromogenic colour print
27.2 x 34.3cm
January 1989
Gabor Szilasi
CCA

*Partial view of the north elevation
at the centre line*
Chromogenic colour print
47.5 x 59.6cm
November 1988
Richard Pare
CCA

Entrance Court details
Chromogenic colour print
47.6 x 59.2cm
January 1989
Richard Pare
CCA

*View of the Entrance Court and West Rotunda,
looking south*
Chromogenic colour print
59.6 x 47.6cm
January 1989
Richard Pare
CCA

*View of Special Collections Study Room and
Scholars' offices, looking northeast*
Chromogenic colour print
59.6 x 47.6cm
November 1988
Richard Pare
CCA

*Partial view of south elevation and Scholars'
Wing with cornice under construction*
Chromogenic colour print
34.3 x 27.2cm
November 1988
Richard Pare
CCA

*View of Library Court and reading rooms,
looking northeast*
Chromogenic colour print
27.2 x 34.3cm
January 1989
Gabor Szilasi
CCA

The long galleries
Chromogenic colour print
34.5 x 27.2cm
January 1989
Gabor Szilasi
CCA

Partial view of offices, curatorial level
Chromogenic colour print
27.2 x 34.5cm
December 1988
Gabor Szilasi
CCA

*Southeast corner of exhibitions workspace,
curatorial level, showing partially glazed
interior window*
Chromogenic colour print
25.3 x 33.1cm
December 1987
Gabor Szilasi
CCA

Corridor, collections vault level
Chromogenic colour print
27.2 x 34.6cm
November 1988
Gabor Szilasi
CCA

Compact storage shelving in archives vault
Chromogenic colour print
27.2 x 34.6cm
December 1988
Gabor Szilasi
CCA

CCA *Garden and south window reflected in glazed
north wall of Scholars' Wing*
Chromogenic colour print
47.6 x 59.6cm
November 1988
Richard Pare
CCA

Fenestration study
Chromogenic colour print
34.3 x 27.2cm
December 1988
Gabor Szilasi
CCA

*View of the south elevation showing Shaughnessy
House and Scholars' Wing, looking east*
Chromogenic colour print
27.2 x 34.2cm
January 1989
Gabor Szilasi
CCA